Women
in Aikido

Women
in Aikido

Andrea Siegel

Photographs by
Jan Watson

North Atlantic Books
Berkeley, California

Women in Aikido

Published by
North Atlantic Books
2741 Eighth Street
Berkeley, California 94710

This is issue #47 in the *Io* series.

Cover photograph by Schuyler Pescada
All interior photographs by Jan Watson
Cover and book design by Paula Morrison
Typeset by Catherine Campaigne
Printed in the United States of America

Women in Aikido is sponsored by The Society for the Study of Native Arts and Sciences, a nonprofit educational corporation whose goals are to develop an educational and crosscultural perspective linking various scientific, social and artistic fields; to nurture a holistic view of arts, sciences, humanities, and healing; and to publish and distribute literature on the relationship of mind, body and nature.

Library of Congress Cataloging-in-Publication Data
Siegel, Andrea, 1963–
    Women in Aikido / Andrea Siegel.
      p.   cm.
    ISBN 1–55643–161–9
    1. Aikido.   2. Martial artists—United States—Interviews.
  3. Self-defense for women.   I. Title.
GV1114.35.S56   1993
796.8'154'0820973—dc20   93–183
                                            CIP

1 2 3 4 5 6 7 8 9 / 97 96 95 94 93

In Memory of My Father
Joseph Peter Siegel
1933–1975

Contents

Introduction

Why women aikido black belts? I wanted to speak with people who have had reason to give a more than cursory examination of the power they wielded, and its purpose. Female experts in a traditionally male, physically rigorous, martial discipline are the exception rather than the rule. I had a hunch that discussions with women who were physically powerful might yield information about power applicable to any domain where issues of mastery and dominance are at stake. This was confirmed by a graduate student reading the first draft of this book who said, "I could substitute Ph.D. for black belt and be reading about me."

The black belt, in this culture, has a mystique, and carries with it the implication of mastery. For my purposes, it was an arbitrary if useful cutoff point. There are so many good women aikidoists that I had an enormous backup list of people I couldn't interview because of space constraints.

Why aikido? As a martial art, it seems to embody many of the paradoxes which I was interested in exploring. A fuller explanation of aikido is in the brief introduction to names and terms at the end of this introduction.

I wanted specifically to discuss several things:

1. What are the interrelationships among power, heart, and common sense? How are these qualities experienced when a woman also has an integrated awareness of her physical body? What results from this kind of awareness?

2. As women enter the public sector in unprecedented numbers, they are developing their power in order to do the best job possible. In this process, a relationship with a mentor, who

is often male, can have a pivotal influence. The novice/mentor relationship is not a new one. But respectfully and carefully dealing with the complications that arise from intensely coaching (or being coached by) a person whom one is potentially attracted to deserves fresh consideration. In the context of aikido, this led me to question: What are the appropriate uses of power and sexuality? And what can be learned from mistakes made when they get confused? What is this phenomenon of "giving one's power away," and how can one get one's power back?

3. While talking with a car salesman, I mentioned this book. He said, "They're probably all really angry at men and do martial arts to get revenge, huh?" I answered, "No. Consistently they tell me that their practice is a search for peace within themselves, and a way to deal with the world that has dignity." He paused a moment and said, "Oh, it's a spiritual practice." (I didn't buy the car.)

   These black belt women seemed to have delved into, and developed for themselves, something far deeper and more rewarding than the joys of mashing another person's face into the ground. What do they get from training? What does it mean when an art of war becomes a spiritual practice?

4. What happens when a woman knows in a fundamental way that she can protect herself physically as well as, or better than, any man can? How does this change the way she perceives herself and her life? And is her world view different from that of us everyday people who go through life sensibly alert, but without those skills that come with a black belt?

5. "What do women want?" is a cry frequently heard in the media, issuing from the mouths of men. The subtext of the question implies that my desires are alien and unknowable, and that the process of trying to understand me fills another group of people with frustration and despair. The people I interviewed answered the question "What do I want?" in inventive, responsible, and integrity-filled ways.

It is not my aim that people read this book and decide to practice aikido. Quite the contrary: the martial art which I have experienced as heartbreakingly beautiful, can at times also be bone-breakingly painful. Any other discipline, or just living itself, seems to be a more sensible exercise. I think integrity is the most valuable thing to practice, and it has a distinct "smell" to it. My hope is that you'll read this and become more familiar with that scent and with the pitfalls of the pursuit, and from that awareness be able to better recognize your own authentic passions and drives when they are calling, and follow them creatively and happily in your life.

❄   ❄   ❄

When someone at a crafts fair mentioned the idea of doing a book of interviews with women aikido black belts, I thought, "What fun!" I talked about it with my friend, Lee, who was perusing the booths with me, and then promptly forgot about it. Toward the end of the day, she said, "Your face lit up when we spoke about that book, and I don't know if I've ever seen you look so happy."

I tend to forget my own happiness, unless reminded. Her reminder hit a deep place in me, and I decided to do this book. I put it on hold until after my aikido blue belt exam (a barely-beyond-beginner test), after which a friend quipped, "You now know enough to be a danger to yourself, but you're not yet a danger to anyone else." After I passed the exam, I started the project.

I had the opportunity to do this book because when my grandfather died he left me enough money to quit my regular job for awhile. I put the money aside, and six years later, when the idea of this book presented itself, I cheerfully offered my employer my resignation. To Grandpa Sidney I owe great thanks.

Parts of this book, or, to be fair, much of this book reflects my own idiosyncrasies. My focus was on understanding each woman's individual process. I love to have stories told to me; it was a privilege to sit with each of these women, ask very direct personal questions, and listen to their frank responses. Each moment of producing this book gave me the joy of having nothing to answer to but my own curiosity. I am delighted to share it with you and I hope you enjoy it.

I was less interested in having this book be discussion-oriented, so my opinions, which ran rampant through the interviewing, were edited out in the bookmaking. Where our discussions forward the action, I've left them in, but for the most part, what's important to this book is the unique perspective of these individuals. I step in briefly in an introduction to each interview to provide a context.

Some Aikido Background Information, and an In-depth Introduction to Names and Terms

Aikido was developed by a 20th-century Japanese martial arts expert named Morihei Ueshiba who studied martial arts his entire life. He wanted to find a way to disarm an attacker without causing harm. He developed a philosophy which addressed this desire; and, culling information from different martial arts, he developed responses to attacks which accomplished this, and taught them to others. He died of cancer in 1969 at the age of 86.

Aikido is a "soft form" martial art. It is unlike the martial arts one usually sees in movies, where it seems that the purpose is to effortlessly maim and perhaps kill people in a *randori* (multiple-person attack situation), or kill people who just happen to be in the neighborhood. In these movies, martial arts skill is presented as a way to become an effective violence-producing machine.

In the U.S. especially, the martial arts can attract a certain type of fearful individual (usually one who has not resolved issues of psychological and/or physical abuse perpetrated against them in childhood) who desires to use self-defense skills to bully or even harm others. This sort of character, unfortunately quite common, has given martial arts a distasteful reputation.

Many other people use the martial arts for *budo* or *bujitsu* (the way of the spiritual warrior). They are seeking on a physical level to protect the innocent, on a philosophical level to take a stand to create a world where violence is no longer necessary, and on a psychological level to heal the violence in their own souls.

The forms of aikido embody this latter philosophy to a great extent. In the aikido *dojo* (training hall), one trains to meet the force of the *uke* (the attacker, literally "the one who takes the fall") in a way that safely "blends" with their *ukemi* (attack, literally "falling away from harm") and disarms the person with the force of their own energy. "Blending"—an essential component of aikido philosophy and action—involves sensing the direction and intensity of the attack and turning to move with it or redirect it. Debate rages about whether what works for the microcosm works for the macrocosm, but it would seem that the effectiveness of blending brings into question the relative ineffectiveness of the predominant "blow for blow" model of conflict resolution, upon which the current world order is based. Regardless, a successful resolution to a dangerous situation leaves both *uke* and *nage* (one who throws the attacker or "receives" the attack) unharmed, with the violent situation completely de-fused. Often the attacker has been thrown (sent flying through the air—much training is spent on learning how to "fly" safely and land well) or pinned (held to the ground so he or she cannot move). In a typical class, the *sensei* (teacher) will show the students the move, and then the students take turns playing the roles of *uke* and *nage*. I'll call out, *"Sensei!"* while I'm training to ask the teacher for help. I find it useful when I am not at my home *dojo*, because I don't easily remember people's names.

In aikido much time is spent developing the "unseen" aspects of the successful management of conflict. The key aspect is called *ki* in Japanese. Roughly defined, it is subtle and maneuverable creative aliveness: the joy-giving substance that flows through all of us. It is similar to the Chinese notion of *chi,* the Hindu notion of *prana,* or the Greek Heraclitean notion of the River. The theory behind *ki*-flow as developed by many people, including the founder Morihei Ueshiba (who is referred to as O'Sensei, meaning the "great teacher"), asserts that there is a universal and overwhelmingly powerful good which we can physically tap into. By authentically connecting with this power, we become capable of preventing harm in a martial context, and creating good in our lives.

In aikido, other ideas are used to help support the development of *ki*-awareness. The concept of *hara* (the center of the body, located approximately three inches below the navel) is used as a focus point to help people drop their attention from the mind to a more embodied awareness, and hence a greater consciousness of the flow of *ki*. This is also called the "center," and "centeredness" is another word for this kind of practice.

Sometimes *ki-ai*-ing (letting forth a burst of sound that comes naturally from deep within the belly, *ki* meaning energy, *ai* meaning shout) is used to develop a sense of sound emanating from a deep place in oneself, more centralized than the vocal cords. This also stimulates the flow of *ki*.

Working with the concept of *ma-ai* (the correct and most comfortable distance between the attacker and the person who receives the attack) is used as a way to discover one's limits. Training in this area gives a martial artist an intuitive sense of when a situation is out of balance, providing them with the uncanny ability to resolve potentially violent situations long before they become dangerous.

Working with *irimi* (entering), one develops the ability to go into an out-of-balance situation fully centered, alive, and aware. One interviewee compared it to experiencing oneself as the still eye of a hurricane.

Like any community, even one with such idealistic motives, the aikido community is not without its political problems. The body of this book does not address these problems. Women from different schools have been interviewed, because everyone has something good to contribute. As an example of the political rifts, as an interviewee summarized, "There's this whole stupid rivalry between Iwama (O'Sensei's Japan country *dojo*) and Hombu (O'Sensei's Japan city *dojo*). It's ridiculous, and I try not to give it too much attention or energy." O'Sensei perhaps contributed to these problems: it is said that near the time of his death, he saw his students one by one, and told each of them that they alone understood the true aikido, and that it was their job to bring the message of aikido into the world. As another interviewee said, "The problem is, they all believed him."

On a more mundane level, certain other terms used in aikido are mentioned in this book. In some *dojos, seiza* (sitting on one's knees, with one's spine fairly straight) is the formal way to sit down on the mat while not doing aikido. It is also the position teachers sit in while evaluating belt exams.

Japanese terms are also used for movements and workout gear. One type of strike is the *shomen* (an overhead strike to the middle of the forehead with the blade part of one's hand—tip of pinky to just above the wrist bone, that fleshy edge). There are many other types of strikes to practice with, such as punches and grabs. The two-step is a way of quickly turning around which is sometimes used repetitively as a warm-up. Some *dojos* do extensive weapons training with the *bokken* (wooden sword) and the *jo* (five-foot-long wooden staff). Frequently, training with swords is also done in *katas* (solo routines). While training, people usually wear a *gi* (a uniform: a top which ties closed and drawstring-waist trousers). Women can also wear a *hakama* (usually dark blue or black long split skirt) at any time they wish to. Men only wear a *hakama* if they have a black belt.

The belt ties the uniform together, but it is also used as a way to denote the wearer's level of experience. In the United States, in many aikido *dojos,* a beginner wears a white belt. After the beginner has successfully completed two tests, she may wear a blue belt. After successful completion of two more tests, she may wear a brown belt. And after passing two more tests, she wears a black belt.

All the pre-black belt tests are called *kyu* tests. When I first started studying aikido, and I heard people referring to their "Q-Tips," I was mystified. Later I found out they were talking about ranking, not cotton swabs. *Kyu* tests are referred to by number (*ikkyu* or "first *kyu*" is the last test before the black belt test, *nikkyu* or "second *kyu*" is the second-to-last test before the black belt test, etc.). All the black belt tests are called *dan* tests. In the U.S., the "average" amount of time it takes to get a first degree black belt is three to five years. I know women who have gotten it in two years, and who have gotten it in ten. The black belts are referred to by number (*shodan* is first degree black belt, *nidan* is second degree, *sandan* is third degree, and so on).

The mystique of the black belt is a Western construct. In Japan, a beginner wears a white belt. Usually after about a year of practice, one tests for a black belt. Outside Japan, the meaning of the test and the degree to which the mystique has value varies for each individual. Often a person is awarded rank because she has successfully passed a test given by her teacher. The number of techniques she must know increases with each test. Frequently, even if she practices the martial arts intensely, the black belt is not acquired for many years. Sometimes rank is given in the absence of testing, for a variety of reasons.

✿　　✿　　✿

The women interviewed mention several teachers, among them Robert Nadeau, Pat Hendricks, Terry Dobson, Frank Doran, and Chiba Sensei. I left the names the way the interviewees used them. If a teacher or method is mentioned in the book, that in no way implies an endorsement. Rather, my hope is that through the exploration of certain questions, a more thorough understanding of the interrelationships between power and compassion might emerge.

The
Interviews

Catherine Tornbom

CATHERINE TORNBOM *was born in Moorhead, Minnesota, in 1951. Her family moved to Los Angeles, California, when she was five. Her childhood was spent in Los Angeles. She attended George Williams College in Chicago where she studied sociology and urban history. At the time the interview took place, Catherine worked as an executive in San Francisco. She is married and lives in Mountain View, California, with her husband and two children. Robert Nadeau was her main aikido teacher.*

Venturing into suburbia to interview Catherine, I felt like I had gone to another planet. Here was a neighborhood, with a quadrangle and kids riding around on bicycles. A dog barked enthusiastically in the background. Catherine greeted me at the door. As I was setting up my tape recorder, I was introduced to her husband and her sons, who were on their way out for a few hours so we would have uninterrupted time to talk.

Her home is simply and elegantly furnished. During the interview, I sat on a dark red leather couch in the living room. She sat across from me on a blue velvet upholstered armchair. Exotic masks hung on the white walls. There was a pale rug on the floor.

Catherine first experienced aikido when she was seven years old. Her father was friends with a man who was an importer who had been to Japan and studied aikido. When an introductory aikido class was offered in their area, he persuaded her father and mother to participate and bring the three children. She remembers being impressed that "Here I was, seven years old, and these full-grown Japanese men were only an inch or two taller than me. It was wonderful."

CATHERINE: One time, to demonstrate the power of *ki*, they asked me to be very, very strong, like a board. They placed me across two different people. My father, who's over six feet tall, stood on me. And I was like a board. That demonstration of my own power, even though we know it's more of a gimmick than it is anything of profound depth, left a deep impression with me.

ANDREA: What is the gimmick?

CATHERINE: It's a game of focusing attention to make your arm or your body unbendable. It is a rather superficial demonstration of something that can be much greater.

After the class ended, she didn't study aikido again until she graduated from college. After graduation, she had the time, the income, and the inclination to pick it back up. She started studying again for a few reasons: a desire to learn self-defense, that memory from the past, and the introduction she'd had to things that weren't seen but could be demonstrated (like making oneself as strong as a board). She looked in the phone book. She called, visited, and said, "OK. How do I sign up?" She was on the mat the next night.

CATHERINE: That was pre-husband, pre-mortgage. That was pre-everything. I could train every night. Almost immediately I traveled to other *dojos* to be exposed to different styles. I'd go to Santa Cruz for a couple of hours, and come back again just for training.

At the time, in the early seventies, women were just beginning to explore empowerment. We'd have women's retreats. Sometimes the women were the roughest to train with because they didn't know what to do with their newfound power. "What do you do with this stuff?" one would ask, and then execute a wrenching, muscle-based technique.

Another would respond: "Well, don't do that because you can seriously hurt me. Let's soften it a little," and then she'd execute an extremely powerful energy-based technique.

The *ki-ai*, a stylized expression of energy through sound, was another challenge for us, unaccustomed to expressing strength through the voice. With our higher-pitched voices, we weren't really

sure where this sound should originate from, much less how to access any depth of powerful expression. We'd say, *"Ee, ee."* We'd look at each other and say, "You can express more than that."

In 1979, she gave birth to Arren. She had trained up until she was about seven months pregnant, and then she took a break.

CATHERINE: Aikido became an internally focused practice for me during the time period prior to Arren's birth. The pregnancy was the start of a process that challenged me profoundly. My body was involved in a powerful, primal process over which I had no control. My body knew exactly what to do to grow that baby, and there was nothing I could say, think, or do to interfere with it. I could cause problems by resisting. Nothing other than going with it can be done with the birth process. It has been that way for millennia. It was absolutely earth-shattering to realize that I was not in control. I am in control of my own thought patterns, but that needed to be differentiated from the forces in the universe.

There was one other aikido woman pregnant at that time. As far as I know, we were the first of that generation of aikidoists to have babies. It changed the feeling in the *dojo* to have a newborn baby present during class. Arren always came with me when he was very young.

ANDREA: How did Arren's being there affect you?

CATHERINE: It added yet another dimension to my aikido. I was committed to responding to my child wholeheartedly and not short-changing any aspect of child rearing. So, when he would let me know I was needed, it meant I would get off the mat and breastfeed until he was done. Sometimes I was resentful because I wanted to complete a technique and I'd think, "I just breastfed you, now it's my turn to train. I don't want to hold you right now. Don't you understand?" And no, he didn't understand. It's completely a one-way route.

Given my commitment to respond to his needs, I thought, "Maybe I can blend more than I ever realized possible." I saw that for me to relate to my child the way I wanted to required that I let go of my preconceived thoughts and patterns of relating to people (especially a baby). Some of the process felt really painful. Everything that was familiar was shifting and changing. But the wonder of it was that I could sense the possibility of new ways of relating and blending with another person.

Words sound a bit hollow, but using the framework of aikido, I find that it gives me that same sense of possibility: there's so much more here than I can even begin to comprehend. There are energies that I can't see, but sometimes I can feel them, and sometimes

I sense them. Rarely can I articulate them or manifest them. The longer I stay with aikido, the more I comprehend and the more I realize how little I understand. I sometimes despair I'm ever going to get the level I'm after. Other times, I think, "Oh! look at the level I just reached. It feels so original, as if it is the first time anyone's ever had this awareness." Never mind that monks in the fifteenth century were having these same awarenesses.

Catherine had been a brown belt, eligible theoretically to take her black belt years before she did it. She took the test in 1980. It was several months after the birth of her firstborn.

ANDREA: Did your black belt test mean anything to you?

CATHERINE: Giving birth was more significant, but I felt that the test represented a rite of passage. Until I took that test I hadn't really pushed myself to the aikido edge and been willing to take the leap. I asked a man named Robbie Long to be my *uke.* I chose him because in my view, he always pushed the edges, the boundaries. In a way he was an unlikely choice since most people want an *uke* who will help them look pretty and give the test a well-rehearsed look. While my ego would have preferred that, I knew by choosing Robbie, the test would be honest. He wouldn't let me get away with any subtle inner games. He'd know when I was trying to hide, when I was not going to give everything I could, and when I was afraid to try. He wouldn't accept a superficial answer or a superficial technique. We both started aikido about the same time and he had received his black belt a year or so earlier.

He also told me to stop telling my child not to holler. He said, "Let him use his voice. See how hard it is for you to use yours?" I thought, "I guess there is a relationship there." So, there was my child, playing on the mat, hollering his head off. I'd be trying to train for my black belt, and my *uke* was pushing me, attacking, and saying, "Come on, you can dig deeper." And my husband agreeing while attacking from the other side.

Faced with the intensity of their attacks, I would draw on inner resources I usually didn't use. My response would then appropriately match the depth of their attack.

Working with him caused me to confront and get out of the safety zone. I'd do a nice, safe form. The one I was taught. I put this toe here and then I put this toe back over here, and then I extend thusly with my arms out that way. He'd say, "Bullshit. What is this?" And then he'd grab me and get on his knees, do something weird, and say "Now do it!" I'd think, "What?!" Part of me would want to say, "Stop acting foolish." Another part of me would say, "I'll show him." Another part of me would be intrigued: "Hmmm. There's probably a different way to do it." And then I'd try to do it differently. Sometimes he'd get angry at me because he knew I was being wishy-washy. He'd say, "Come on, I know there's more in there. What is this? This is an insult to me." And then I'd say, "RRRRHHH." My muscles started popping a little, and I'd feel a little extra heaviness in my legs, and I'd walk with more purpose. He'd scream, "RAHHH," and I'd match it by screaming "ARHHHH."

He was trying to draw out of me what I didn't see, was scared to acknowledge, or what flat-out frightened the shit out of me. I asked, "But what happens when you're that strong?" He'd say, "I don't know. Let's play with it." I'd respond, "That's easy for you to say. I don't know if I want to play with it." Those issues haven't changed. But, today, they're played out at different levels. There are important ones that I have to continue looking at in different ways to make sure I'm still moving forward. It's difficult to take a step backward—too hard-earned to go backward. I don't ever want to go backward. It was an amazing process, and I'm thankful I did it that way. I learned a lot.

The test was one of the last big tests among all the schools. All the big main guys were there. They were sitting *seiza*. A hand is on each knee. And they are looking Buddha-like, but not in a smiling stance. Not giving away anything. Their faces are stone. Furthermore, they're going to sit *seiza* for the entire time even if they lose the entire lower part of their body. They won't let on. They go numb from sitting *seiza*. I can't sit more than for five minutes, and then I've lost my legs.

I held Arren, and then gave him to my husband, Harvey, but not very well. I was so nervous. I said, "Here. You've got to take him now." Startled at my sudden thrusting of him away, Arren started to cry. I'm walking out on the mat on my knees, which is the traditional way to start. I'm kind of in shock. The whole thing is a very shocking experience. The pressure's on my knees, and I can't breathe. I don't think I ever found my center. My *uke* kept attacking me, and I kept getting hit. Fortunately, videos weren't big then. I just have still shots. Stills never look as bad as a video. I hadn't allowed that much juice to come through my system since I was a child.

That came up from the moment I started. It built more and more. At first, I felt some semblance of control. But the longer I was out there, the more my breath became labored. So much came up, I didn't know what the hell to do with it. It was the first demonstration of just how much energy I could draw up. I didn't know how to accept it. I got through the multiple-person attack. I still tend to clamp down on that much energy coming through. I've only experienced it a couple of times since. It was frightful for me. I always question: "What will I do when that much energy comes through?"

Being fearful about energy coming through is a misunderstanding. I had a very abusive childhood. That has motivated me toward appropriate expression of physical energy. I knew that when that much energy came through, that's the kind of energy I could kill with. I misunderstood what energy means. For me, it was violence and anger. All my years of going through certain kinds of physical therapies, emotional therapies, and then aikido, was to inch-(and I mean inch) by-inch relearn a pattern so that the energy is the energy.

ANDREA: "The energy is the energy" as separate from what?

CATHERINE: Whatever emotional impact, interpretation, or misunderstanding I put on it. The energy that comes through can be the most profound expression of love or the most profound expression of cruelty. It's the same energy. One time, I said to my teacher, "I'm really scared. I know how abusive powerful energy can be. What guarantee do I have that I'm not going to slip on the mat? I've hurt people before. Fortunately not very seriously, but inappropriate energy coming through is dangerous."

And he said, "I can't give you what you want. There are no guarantees." OK, I know that, but I still want to ask every once in a while. Please, can I have a guarantee? Can I have some safety? Can I be OK?

ANDREA: When you finished your test, was Harvey still holding the baby?

CATHERINE: It was a bit of a blur after that. I went back and held Arren, who was still upset, and said, "I'm so sorry, but I had this test."

Terry Dobson, another instructor, was there. I wanted his feedback on my test. He said, "You're beautiful. You were completely yourself." I thought, "Oh, God. How embarrassing." I was grateful because he didn't do what is so typical in those situations and tear apart the technique, "She didn't dahdahdah, but she did this well. That's not so important, but this is." He was looking at my total self-expression. I remember that was because that was an affirmation. About that time, I had started losing interest in form. I wanted comprehension of the energy aspect. I was thinking, "What is this energy that I can't see, sometimes I feel, that I get the effects of? When it's done the certain way that I like, it's a really special experience. And it's not like anything else."

What it isn't is force. It's not jarring, and it's not inappropriate. It feels like the most appropriate, physical place for my body to be. It's the most appropriate emotional space. In a spiritual sense, the image is sometimes the most dark, big, and nourishing space possible. Sometimes it's incredibly bright, very light—a large tunnel in which I move. It seems like the only way that one can go in the universe. It hits me on those levels. If a person throws me in that space of being so perfectly blended, in that energy space, the fall feels absolutely effortless. Some aikido falls can be so jarring. They all have the potential to end in a painful splat. Yet, when I'm lined up, my hands, my body parts, my knees, everything's in the right place. Sometimes there's a momentary blank. I feel that I was in a very special nonphysical space, in and out of it. There's almost amnesia. I don't remember anything else around me for that moment. Then I think, "Wow. Can I go there again? It felt great."

One of the ways that I see this in my daily life has to do with my view of spirituality. For me, the spiritual practice is the most important. I know that there's a route of oneness, and my maintaining any illusion of separateness from the whole is just plain dysfunctional. I can't maintain the illusion that, in separateness, I can move with integrity. I'm deeply touched if I'm just sitting here, whether you are here or not, whether my kids are here or not, whether my employees are working or not, my parents, my family, any of my aikido. And it keeps moving out into my community more and more.

ANDREA: After your test, what did you do?

CATHERINE: For a time, my husband and I lived in Austin, Texas, due to a job transfer, and we both taught and trained. In Austin, a serendipitous meeting occurred. A highly ranked aikido teacher came through Austin to do a special training class. Harvey and I and another teacher went out to dinner with him. I asked about his background. And he said, "I first came to the U.S. in the early sixties to the Los Angeles area." After exploring his background more, I realized that he was one of those men I trained with twenty-five years ago. I said, "Oh, you've changed a little." He was balding, a little gray. "Well, you've changed, too," he said. I was not the skinny little runt I was at seven.

ANDREA: In Austin, did you teach?

CATHERINE: Yes, but I was ambivalent. I've always hesitated to put myself forward as an aikido teacher. In Austin, because there were so few teachers, I began teaching. Through the recreation services at Bergstrom Air Force Base, I started a class. That was very interesting. I had a lot of opportunity to explore what power meant.

The soldier's mode is very male: there are well-defined, well-structured, appropriate responses and actions for everything. If you don't know what your action is, you go to the manual to discover the action. I wasn't focusing on the martial aspect of aikido. I'm telling them to move in circles, and I'm talking about spirals. They're linear and very rigid. They're probably the most polite group of people I've ever come across. I would say, "Well, do this," and they'd say, "Yes, ma'am."

And they pop up and do it. They were so well trained. Some of the officers seemed quite at home and comfortable with that rigidity. That's probably why they signed up for the long term. Some of the young men who came to my class were trying to figure out what to do with themselves. Quite a few of them had studied martial arts. I would do things that would kind of confound them.

I wouldn't say that I had any really strong skill. I just knew a little bit more about how energy worked, and a couple of them would get into, "Oh, you're a master." I'd say, "No, no, no. We don't do that thing in aikido. No. I'm trying to respond to what's in the moment, and trying to understand what's coming at me. I don't ask 'Why?' because sometimes I don't have that opportunity, but I try to respond in a way that makes the most sense in that situation."

It was a lot of fun, especially when they would attack me with their full strength. On occasion, I would have to explain to them, "If you really want to attack that strongly, we can't do this technique. I'll do something different." I'd show them a different way to respond, and that would blow their minds. Because, in their minds, there's only one, by the book, way to do things. I'd respond, "No matter what, I'm supposed to do that move, when you guys could break my arm if I did it? You know I'm not that strong. You tower over me in height and weight."

I discovered quickly that if I wasn't completely honest with myself, I wasn't going to move them or me anywhere.

ANDREA: What is that honesty that moves them?

CATHERINE: On one level, it's a lack of hype or bravado. Also, I'm not a teacher who says, "You do it and I'll watch." On a physical level, what moves them is whatever I happen to emanate from within that is reflected physically. So I make sure I take deep breaths, and get that physical sense of my body. I seem to get a little heavier. I settle, and then am able to move them in a way they didn't expect. I actually demonstrated what I was trying to say enough so that they knew I had something for them. It was a combination of what I said, what I was doing, and my willingness to admit I've made a mistake. I'd never hesitate to say, "Let's redo that. I realize I'm not saying what I mean. I thought I wanted to do that. But look, it's not working. We need to do something slightly different."

My favorite thing to say now during training and when the technique isn't working is, "Wasn't that a great *thought!* Wouldn't that be heaven?" I've got a partner still looking at me and saying, "Well, what are you going to do?" I think, "Great thought, OK. Let's see if it can integrate into all the other levels that I know, believe, and love, that don't always manifest as much as I want to manifest them."

I also taught a women's aikido class through the Austin Parks and Recreation, and an aikido-based energy class through my church. When I got pregnant with Noel, I pulled way back, and Harvey took the Bergstrom class.

ANDREA: Why did you pull back?

CATHERINE: When I'm pregnant, it becomes a very internal affair, as I mentioned earlier. It's all I can do to acknowledge the extra growth inside. "Sorry, guys," I said, "this is my priority." I had another child in my household, so I pulled back into a fairly classic feminine role, which was more comfortable at the time. We were in Austin for four years. We've been back from Texas for about four years now.

Now, when I train, I get from aikido the very specific feedback that working with a partner provides. It's good to have a philosophy, be very thoughtful, and even construct different realities, but until I get immediate feedback from someone who hasn't necessarily bought into my particular reality, I'm not truly relating or communicating what is the reality for us at that moment. I find that when I acknowledge my body for feedback, I'm much healthier than if I use only my brain, and try to separate the two. Even though I am not focussed on the technique, I'm not worried about whether I'm going to get hit by my partner. Sometimes I am creamed terribly, but that is also important feedback. I think, "Look at that. My hands are clenched. My chest is thrust. My muscles are tensed." The outcome is predictable with that stance.

I use aikido to understand and resolve everyday situations. For example, at work, an employee was trying to undermine me. I decided to work out this situation in aikido and understand my part in it. With certain training partners, I can ask them to help me explore the situation by representing the "problem." As we practiced the technique with this focus, I observed my thoughts and physical reactions. My reaction to my "problem" partner was telling—I tried to turn away, to disassociate. That's what I was doing at work as well. Then I began working on connecting more, trying to stay present no matter what was coming at me.

Sometimes it seems really physical. I literally pull energy out of my arms and my legs. Sometimes it seems more emotional. I'll say I feel so sad or whatever the emotion is. I'll face my partner and focus very intently on my chest, and see what emotions or what thoughts are coming up. Not trying to talk it to death, but say, "Tell me what you perceive." "Gosh," she says, "You're hunched over. Let's look at it." I ask myself, "Can I square my shoulders when I'm feeling that pain in my heart?" Suddenly my lower back hurts. I think, "Can I still feel some strength in my knees? Can I play an aikido game of surging some energy through my body to support that portion that feels a little weak? Why is that weak? What issue haven't I dealt with? Have I got some blinders on?" I depend on my partner to tell me. If she doesn't, aikido becomes as superficial as most everyday acts. My partner says, "Well, when you came in, you really stuck your shoulder out there." Or, "That was great. I've never seen a more perfect technique. But I feel like you really didn't give two hoots about me." If my intention is to give two hoots about her, how do I have perfect form and include her, so she is enriched and empowered?

I tend to be self-centered about the practice. What's it going to do for me? How am I going to push myself to the levels that I want to go to? Aikido helps remind me that I can't do any of that all by myself. I try, but I can't very well effect it in the long or short term.

ANDREA: When looking for people who give true feedback, how do you know you've found someone?

CATHERINE: I can count on one hand the folks that will do it. My husband, Harvey, will. Whenever we train together, I can count on him being right there and telling me. Through the years I've been, in varying degrees, open to it or not. I have some very good friends whom I have encouraged, saying, "It doesn't do me any good if you don't tell me." And, on occasion a random person will give feedback as clear as day. Sometimes it's verbal. Sometimes I'll just know that I need to make a shift. If I'm training with someone, I watch what I'm saying to them. Usually, what I'm correcting in another person's technique is my own issue. Generally, it's true for them, but I'm so acutely in tune with it because it's also mine.

I do a running commentary when I'm training. "Oooh. Did that feel as rough to you as it did to me?" I frequently question, "Was that on or off?" I frequently know when it's off, but I just as frequently I don't know when it's on. Sometimes, I don't trust it. I think, "This doesn't feel like what I might normally do. The range is different."

Sometimes I think, "Oh, wait a minute. I'll make sure my fingers are real alive. I'll make sure my spine goes straight. Am I remembering my hips are there? Do I actually feel some toes on the mat?" I'll do a little check, and then I'll move again. Then I'll think, "God, I'm really scared. I don't know what to do next." Then my partner usually says, "Well, nothing new in this. This is OK." I'll move and say, "God, that's awful. Let's adjust." I'll make an adjustment. I'll finish. Then I'll say, "I liked that part. I want to have this stance and awareness before she even grabs me or attacks." I work it through so I blend with what's happening to me right in the moment, if I can work it through my body.

When I do an effective technique, sometimes I'm surprised by how it feels. I think, "Aren't I supposed to have more control? Aren't I supposed to do something?" I used to hear from my teachers all the time, "Don't do it." And I'd think, "Well, if I don't do it, how does it get done?" With aikido, it's so graphic that "not-doing" is different from passivity. I somehow experience just full presence, openness, and receptivity. I'm being or somehow manifesting what is needed in that moment, with that partner, in that situation.

ANDREA: After that practice, what was different when you faced the person who was undermining you at work?

CATHERINE: Mostly me. As much as I resist it, the point is always for me to adjust, to make the shift. That situation hasn't resolved itself. It involves bringing in a third person to help, and not feeling, "After everything I've done, why can't I do it myself?" I'm working very hard to take the insight I learn from aikido to a level where if I get resentful or angry, I don't act on it.

ANDREA: How do you nourish yourself?

CATHERINE: Not very well right now. I work full-time. I have two children, and a husband. They all have activities. Being a mother of children who are still fairly young, I have a heavy-duty focus to meet their needs. I have full-time help, but that's like another member of the family. She needs nourishment and support, too. I don't always get very well nourished. I have employees at work who I have to deal with. I have to respond to the people above me.

I use Jazzercise as one of my nurturances. It's the physical outlet for me. It gives me the warm-ups and the flexibility. It gets the heart going. Speaking of which, I didn't get to go this morning because I needed to get tires on the car. In my life, there are constant trade-offs. I can't ever count on any one thing in any one week.

I've gone through periods of being a vegetarian. Being pregnant changed that to flat-out carnivore. Do you remember *Rosemary's Baby*? When she was eating a raw steak, I thought, "I recognize that." I have found that I really cannot do well without meat. It's a balance. Maybe if I evolve later. . . . I eat a lot of vegetables and fruits. I'm basically off sugar of any form except as it appears in ketchup and stuff like that. No caffeine. I never drink alcohol. I numb myself enough with my own inner process. I don't need any externals.

The other time I grab: I work in San Francisco, I live on the Peninsula, and I take the train. The hour in the morning, and hour in the afternoon coming back are mine. I either sleep, or I meditate.

The other thing that I do to nourish myself, is walk from the train station to my office, which is about a mile. I have a little tape deck and I listen to different kinds of tapes. Now, I'm listening to "Coping with Difficult People." It's so superficial, but on some level, those tools are helpful. It helps to augment the deep metaphysical things I'm doing, which are difficult to ground in this world.

I try to stick in moments: for some time now I have been training early on Sunday morning with a good friend, Mary Tabor. The two of us delve in and work on various dynamics at a deeper level than can usually be done during a regular class. It's very personal and eclectic because we spend a lot of time expressing and feeling the energy but the form is still recognizable.

ANDREA: When you mentioned mortgages earlier, you almost made it sound like a spiritual path.

CATHERINE: It's a big deal. It signals maturity, or at least a willingness to have a certain kind of lifestyle. It has to do with a level of responsibility. The word "mortgage" says, "Here I am being an adult. I have to do my budget and be thoughtful."

ANDREA: Before we got on tape, you were making fun of how suburban you are. In fact, that's a way of expressing something else?

CATHERINE: It's my style of being grounded. There's a certain level of comfort here that I need to take the risks that I need to take to grow.

ANDREA: What do you mean by comfort, and then what do your risks become?

CATHERINE: My comfort has to do with my physical surroundings: not simply the house where I live, but also comfort has to do with my feeling comfortable in me. My comfort level has to do with having certain basics taken care of, like the schools my children go to, and the classes they take, the neighborhood we live in.

At this point a dog barked in the background, as if to chime in his approval.

CATHERINE: Then, the risk for me is, "What can I do emotionally to break out of the patterns, the attitudes, the wrong thinking, the misunderstandings?" This physical environment helps me to do this. I find this curious because this form can be also quite confining. I can be very comfortable here, and ignore the rest of the world.

"There's no relation to me. Look at my nice house." But by its very calm nature, I can then go out into a bit more chaos. The more I know, the less I can get away with trying to go through life being untouched or not challenged. When I get too comfortable, I think, "Yawn. Whoa! What's the thrill in this? There's no thrill. Let's move. Let's get things moving."

Also a part of my upbringing is expecting a certain kind of life standard. For a very short time after college I played out being footloose and kind of hippie-like. I also had to act out my feminist macha stuff. I worked for Pacific Gas & Electric as a hard hat doing construction work. All 5'2" and 100 pounds. But it was a great time while I did it.

ANDREA: Some people can't find the place where meaningful work and income meet. You seem to have struck a balance. How?

CATHERINE: I simply will accept no less. I will not live that way. It was a very conscious striving. My goal is that my income matches what I want to do. When I line up behind a goal, it happens. I have that certainty.

ANDREA: It sounds like something inborn.

CATHERINE: I think so. A lot of the people who come to aikido seem to be part of the counterculture regarding lifestyle and material possessions.

ANDREA: Do you feel safe in the world?

CATHERINE: I do. The area I walk through from the train station to my office is peopled by some of the most destitute in San Francisco. I walk with purpose. I walk so that I have a great deal of connection to the ground. I sense my body working in unison with all its parts. I feel the musculature. I feel strong and ready to move.

Drivers are pretty aggressive. They don't always obey the law about pedestrians having the right of way. The other day, I was in the middle of a crosswalk and a driver didn't see me. He made a wild turn directly toward me. He was fast. Just for a moment, I paused, and his car passed by, just missing me.

He saw me in his rearview mirror and started to panic, and I thought, "That was close." I watched my reaction. No adrenalin. No anger, just a matter-of-fact acknowledgment of the situation. I just kept walking. I looked at him. I just shrugged my shoulders and kept walking. He was traumatized. In my system, there wasn't a stop, but rather that sense of ebb and flow, and I don't worry about it much.

In the background we could hear the sound of the garage door opening; her family had returned home.

ANDREA: Is there anything else you'd like to say?

CATHERINE: The ongoing commitment to shift and change is really important. Aikido is a superb tool. A superb method, it doesn't matter the level. To a non-aikido person reading the book, I would say, "Come and check it out, train for any length of time." Even if a person did it for just a short time, the lessons learned are profound and will stay.

As we were wrapping up the interview, her younger son ran in and made a Dracula face at me. He'd fashioned fangs out of cropped soda straws. He then ran to his mom, who gave him a hug.

Several months after this interview took place, Catherine resigned from her job to start her own business—a multi-association management company.

Lorraine DiAnne

LORRAINE DIANNE, *a fifth degree black belt, is one of the three top-ranked women aikidoists in the United States. She began studying aikido in 1970 at the age of nineteen when she was at the University of Massachusetts at Amherst. After six years of training in the United States, she and her then husband moved to Japan to study to become aikido teachers. In Japan, she trained roughly six hours a day, seven days a week, for three years, at which point her main teacher, Chiba Sensei, told her she was ready to return to the United States to start her career as a teacher. She taught at Aikido of Berkeley in California for two-and-a-half years, and now has her own dojo in Springfield, Massachusetts.*

In February of 1989, I'd just started doing aikido. I was accustomed to training in a small basement room with a half-dozen people. Friends invited me to watch black-belt tests at a local dojo. I walked into an old converted warehouse with high wood-beamed ceilings and huge opaque windows through which streamed the setting sun. On the large expanse of mat, to the right of a golden wood altar, sat Lorraine DiAnne. She was sitting in seiza, in the line of highly ranked judges of the exam. She appeared graceful, imperturbable, upright, formidable. (I didn't know that teachers often assume, during tests, an intensity and seriousness of expression which doesn't necessarily show up in daily life.) After watching the exams, I went home and scribbled furiously about how strong an impression this had made upon me. To speak with her for this book, I called someone in Santa Cruz, who gave me the phone number of someone in Ottawa, who gave me her address in Massachusetts. The interview took place over the phone.

Lorraine described her surroundings: "I'm speaking on the phone from my bedroom. It's evening, 7 PM, so the shades are drawn. On the walls around me are Japanese woodblocks and paintings. The only light in the room is a small Japanese-style rice paper lamp sitting on the end table next to the bed. The bed itself is a futon with a host of pillows for me to prop myself up in a comfortable position for the conversation to come. On the bed beside me, with his head in my lap, is Kojiro, my hundred-pound Akita (Japanese dog)."

ANDREA: Do you feel safe in the world?

LORRAINE: I do. It may not be real. It may all be in my mind. People have said to me that when I walk around, they're very aware of me, and the feeling that I put out of calmness, and awareness of everything. They feel they could never sneak up on me.

A few months ago, a drunk ex-friend of mine broke into my house, and tried to physically assault me. He wasn't able to at all. I was quite able to take care of myself.

ANDREA: Did you call the police?

LORRAINE: Yes. They told me there wasn't a patrol car available, and there wouldn't be one for twenty minutes. I said, "What do you mean?"

"We can't send anybody for twenty minutes."

"What am I supposed to do? Sit down and have tea with this man who's trying to punch me out? You need to send someone here."

"Well, you're going to have to wait twenty minutes to a half an hour," they said. I said, "If you're going to take that long, send an ambulance because he'll need it." And I hung up. I was very angry.

In five minutes, they had two patrol cars here. And in that way, they were very quick to respond to the fact that I was saying that I was going to defend myself. But I had a feeling of helplessness because when the police came, they said, "Did he try to hit you?"

"Yes."

"Did he hit you?"

"No," I said.

"Well, then we can't file anything."

I said, "You mean because I made the effort to learn how to defend myself I can't file against someone who tried to attack me and brought violence into my house?"

ANDREA: What did you do to make your place yours again?

LORRAINE: I had dated a couple of cops. I called them and expressed what I was feeling. Then, I asked what they thought was coming from the other side, why I was treated the way I was, and what explanations there could be, so I could try and understand what was going on. I didn't want to hate blindly.

I had already done that. Most of my life I've hated cops. It's only in the last few years that I've realized that they're human beings, too, and I need to understand.

They also thought this should not have happened the way it did. But, they said, there are a lot of cases where the woman calls, she's being beat up, they come, they arrest the guy, and the woman starts hitting the cops with stuff because she doesn't want him taken away. It's very frustrating for them.

In Massachusetts they've now got a new law that if they're called, they have to make an arrest. It's because of all the false calls that come in. I became a victim of that. I wasn't arrested because this was before the new law. I was a victim of the cops' frustration about false calls. I was given no chance to prove he did not live with me, and I was not going to welcome him in my house the next day.

I talked with a close girlfriend a lot about feelings that it brought up. I talked with one of my senior students about what kinds of emotions it brought up. And then I let it go.

People said, "Did you change your locks? Did you get a weapon?" I didn't change anything. Still, if a friend comes to the door, I'll open the door to talk to them. If they force their way in, I'll deal with it as a separate instance.

I wasn't going to make my life topsy-turvy because someone entered it and created this craziness. That's how I let it go. I haven't seen the person or had anything to do with him whatsoever. I filed a trespassing order, which means that if he ever shows up on my property, they can and will arrest him. I made it clear to him that I never wanted him here again, and then I got on with my life.

ANDREA: That's one kind of danger. Another is the danger of wielding power. In the aikido world, you're a person in a position of power. What is the danger of power?

LORRAINE: Teachers controlling the students' lives. Students come to me to learn. Anything I tell them they need to do to learn, they're willing to do.

Also, if they're going to look up to me, then my life should fit that. I shouldn't tell my students they have to be good, clean, upstanding citizens and then be snorting cocaine on the side and soliciting on the street.

If I only become concerned about self-gratification, I can abuse the power. And I can use them in a way that is not fair to them or to myself. I don't say, "Well, if they give me this power, then I deserve it." I don't trust the power that my students give me. I'm always thinking, "I don't deserve it." I'm very, very hesitant to ever use it, even when I think what I'm doing is right. Also, as long as I stay in tune with my students' feelings and my own emotions, I can't abuse my power.

I say to my students, "When we're within the four walls, I'm *Sensei*. But outside of the four walls, I'm Lorraine. It's real important that you know that, and be able to tell the difference. Don't try to make me into *Sensei* when I'm not supposed to be. And don't make *Sensei* into Lorraine when she's not supposed to be."

That helps. They can see that I'm trying to balance the power. I could be *Sensei* all the time. I did that for awhile. I didn't know I was doing it until people who didn't know anything about the martial arts started telling me, "God, you act like we all owe you something. Like we all have to do the effort to talk to you because you don't go looking to talk to us."

I realized, "Well, I've got to get out of this mode, and find out who I am."

ANDREA: In O'Sensei's teaching, he talked about love. Can you talk about your experiences with that?

LORRAINE: Initially, the concept of love meant that I kind of floated through aikido. I did it very lightly. I just had fun.

When I went to Japan, the training was aggressive and very hardcore. At first, I thought, "God, how could you call this love? These people look like they're bashing themselves to death. What's going on here?" And then I started to understand.

When I was attacking Chiba Sensei, one of my teachers, I would be handing him my life. I would want to hit. I attacked with every part of my being. He would then take that, redirect it, and give it back to me. The next thing I knew, I'd be coming out of a fall, standing up, and looking at him. The feeling of elation: "Wow, I survived that," was so wonderful.

To me, that became the expression of love within the aggressive style. I was giving myself, saying, "Here I am. You can take my life if you want it," and he handed it back uninjured, as it was given to him.

Someone watching would say, "Boy, he really beat you up."

But I wouldn't feel I'd been beaten up. I realized, "You can't always judge it from the outside. You have to know what's going on between the two individuals to understand. This is an expression of love. It's what you do in love in a lot of different ways. With friends, you give 100 percent to them to help them, and then when you need it, they give back."

People who do a softer style of aikido usually do not understand what's going on when they watch Chiba Sensei. But, in fifteen years of study, Chiba Sensei has never hurt me. And he's thrown me a lot. With other teachers, whenever I lose that sense of trust, I get hurt. As long as I maintain it, I never seem to get hurt.

By trust, I mean feeling good about giving myself to the person and trusting that they will give it back. When I try to give a gift, but hold back, I get hurt. A gift has to be given completely. It can't be given and taken at the same time. Whatever I do, there will be a return. It's like a mirror: the reflection comes back to me.

But, again, I have to trust that the person I'm studying with is teaching me "the real stuff," and that it really works.

That's why you must pick a teacher carefully. If you can't trust that person on the mat, they shouldn't be your teacher. If you can

trust them, then follow what they're telling you. You can't go wrong as long as you do that.

You also need to follow what your body tells you. If you're an older student coming in, don't try to do what the teenagers are trying to do. Don't try to be flashy. Feel your body. Notice what it's willing to do, and what it's not willing to do, and work within that framework.

ANDREA: How did you come to study aikido?

LORRAINE: When I attended college at the University of Massachusetts in Amherst, I decided I needed self-defense. I did judo for about a year and a half, and got fed up with the competitiveness of it and the attitudes of a lot of the men who taught. I spoke about this with the chief instructor, who I really liked, and he said, "I think you'd like aikido. Switch to that."

I signed up for an aikido class and fell in love with it from day one. I thought, "This is what I want to do." Initially I didn't care if I learned to throw people, but I wanted to be able to fly through the air and do those falls. Slowly, I also started liking the throws and the discipline.

My first teacher, Tai Unno, was a professor of religion at Smith College, and a fourth degree black belt. He had little stories, and he lived what I perceived as the perfect life. I looked at him, and said, "Yes. I want to be like that." He was supportive of men and women. There was no distinction in his mind. If you came to learn, he taught. As I continued studying, he started taking more and more time off from aikido to do his work at the college. About three years into my practice, I found myself thrust into the role of teacher.

It was fun, but I felt like I was in water over my head. I didn't have answers. I was scared when people questioned things that I did, and became very defensive.

I realized one day that I was going to probably practice aikido for the rest of my life. I might end up someplace where there wasn't a teacher, and maybe I should consider teaching, because I enjoyed it.

I was told that if I wanted to teach it was important that I go to the source, to Japan to train. That scared me. I said, "OK," and didn't think about it for six months. Then I decided, "I guess that's what I should do." My teacher got myself and my husband visas and a sponsor. The next thing I knew, I was in Tokyo.

ANDREA: What was it like for you to study in Japan?

LORRAINE: A lot of the older men black belts initially wanted to help me as they do with all the young women who train. But as I started to get strong, they got more resistant, and told me, "You should do it pretty and gracefully." I was very stubborn, and refused. They would play *ki* games with me.

In other words, if I tried to throw them, they wouldn't budge. I would be frustrated and mad, but I wouldn't give up. Eventually, when they saw that I wasn't going to submit, they backed off, and wouldn't train with me anymore. But they'd send a white-belt male after me. His job was to bash me around, and convince me that this was not how I wanted to train.

I'm not a small person. I'm 5'9" and fairly strong. When they started to beat up on me, I usually could hold my own. I would fight one-to-one on the mat with them. As my technique got better, they were less able to control me. I was literally beating up men on the mat every day.

I'd have to set the limit. They'd come and try to teach me a lesson, and I'd have to bash them to the point where they became afraid to give me any more resistance. Then we could finally train one-on-one. Day after day, there was someone new who thought he could put me in my place.

ANDREA: Where did you get the spirit? It takes a tremendous courage.

LORRAINE: I'm really stubborn. My father told me, "If you want something, you've got it. It doesn't matter if you're a woman or a man. You can get anything you want if you work hard enough at it." I knew I could be whatever I wanted. And I didn't let anybody tell me I couldn't.

I was sort of my father's son. I played very competitive team sports, so I was used to fighting my way through things. So, I kept at it. A lot of times, I'd leave the mat at the end of class, and I'd go out on the fire escape and just cry. It was so frustrating, so hard.

But most of the foreign men who were training there would come to me, and they'd say, "Come on. You can do it. You can fight through it. You'll make it. No problem. You're better than they are. You'll get there." They could see what was going on. There wasn't anything they could do to help. Some of them would take guys aside and beat them up afterwards, but it didn't have the same effect.

I felt like I needed to do it. They needed to learn from me.

The hierarchy shifted back to the older black belts taking me on. Their goal was to try to smash me around, and then not let me throw them. But my technique had gotten to where I could off-balance them. They started having to take falls. It got as frustrating for them as it was for me.

Finally they dismissed me as an oddity, something strange that they didn't want to deal with. They'd ignore me, but that was all right with me. I just didn't train much with Japanese men at all.

ANDREA: What kept you going in aikido?

LORRAINE: When I went to college, my dad gave me the old college talk. He emphasized that being black meant that to achieve I was going to have to be three to four times as good as any white person.

I felt that I only want to be as good as I am. If it's not good enough to make it in this world, then it's not good enough to make it. But I'm not going to kill myself to be four times better than anyone else. I shouldn't have to, and I refuse to do it.

That would have been hard for him to hear. He had done that all his life. It would have been like I was slapping him in the face, and saying, "You've wasted your life." Which was not what I meant at all. So I never actually confronted him with my feelings.

We have a real good relationship. He has always respected me for making and sticking to my convictions. I told him that I either can make it as I am, or I will die trying.

I think that's what kept me going through all the hard times in aikido. I didn't feel I had to be better than everybody else, but they were damn well going to accept me for being as good as I was.

During this time, Lorraine decided she wanted to be a "private student." She thought if she could be a student of someone, he would be able to give her a guideline—very clear things that she needed to work on—and help her understand what was going on. When she first arrived at Hombu dojo in Japan, she found it hard to believe the twelve instructors were doing the same martial art. She couldn't begin to imagine what she should take from each teacher and study.

*She was looking for the thread that tied it all together. After train-
ing for a month and a half, she had a list of three people with whom
she wanted to be a private student. She figured if the first one turned
her down, she'd go to the next.*

*Her first choice was Chiba Sensei, who accepted her right off.
He made several requests of her as his private student: that she stay
in Japan until he decided her training was finished, that she train
under every teacher, that she work only enough to pay her bills (a
lot of money can be made teaching English), and that she study an
additional martial art. She chose a Japanese martial art called Iaido.*

*Once she started training with Chiba Sensei, she was able to find
a connecting thread with the other teachers, who also took her much
more seriously. The word had gone through the school that she was
studying to be a teacher. Because she was a woman, the teachers
would not use her for* ukemi—*as the person with whom they would
demonstrate techniques in front of the class. The first person to use
her for* ukemi *in the front was Chiba Sensei. The next thing she
knew, almost all the teachers used her for* ukemi. *That was a major
breakthrough. Once that happened, her training really began.*

LORRAINE: When they threw me, I could feel what the technique
was supposed to be like. I had something more concrete to deal
with. They were testing me. They'd throw me harder and harder,
trying to find where I would break, not only physically, but emotionally.

Injuries came and went, but I couldn't let them know I was hurt.
Even if they threw me and I got hurt, I'd cover it up. The next day
in class, I'd show up with a bandage on. They'd say, "What happened?"

I'd say, "Oh, I hurt this." I wouldn't say when. I had an advantage in that I was black. The Japanese had rules for Japanese women
and for white women who trained. But there had never been a black
woman training. They didn't know what rules they should hold up
for me.

I got to set my own rules. They said, "Well, we'll see what she
can do, what she can't do." If any other black woman shows up,
she's going to have to live up to what I set up.

I was aware that I was getting the recognition and being thrown around. As a woman, I was real happy about that. At the same time, all through my training, as far back as I can remember, I wanted a role model so badly, some woman who was way ahead of me who I could look to for support and guidance. There just weren't any around.

When I got to Japan, although I looked up to the women who were training there, they weren't given any power within the structure. I found I was starting to be a role model for people, which was scary. I thought, "Oh, God. I can't be a role model. I can't do that. I'm going to fall short. I'm not going to be good enough to be a role model for other people. This is not good."

But I kept training.

ANDREA: Had you tested?

LORRAINE: In Japan, I tested for *shodan* and *nidan*. They were significant events for me, the *shodan* particularly. Chiba Sensei asked the instructors to give me a much more intense test than they did regularly.

In the normal test, maybe you'd do ten or twelve techniques. You'd know what they were very clearly. The test normally took fifteen minutes.

For my test, the teachers would call out an attack, and then I had to keep defending with every technique I could think of. When I'd run out of techniques, they'd call out the next attack. My test took about an hour. It was good for me. Chiba Sensei came to watch. He wasn't going to, and I asked him if he would be there because I was such an emotional wreck.

About halfway through the test, my *uke* (attacker) got scared of me, and wouldn't get up and re-attack me after the fall. The instructors were yelling at him. I got so frustrated that I would throw him down, and then I would pick him up, stand him on his feet, and then I'd throw him down again. It was amusing in a very weird way.

I think that he had never imagined that a woman could throw him as strongly as I was throwing. I'm not saying that I was so amazing, but to him, a woman should be weak. He never imagined that his fall might not be adequate to handle a woman's throw.

It scared him to his roots. He knew every time he got thrown, he was having a hard time. He was losing face. As a result, they failed him on his test. He was testing at the same time. Although he performed his test fine, I think the fact that he was trying to run away from me made him fail.

Lorraine took her nidan *about six months before she left Japan. It wasn't as important a step for her as her* shodan *had been, but it proved that she had gotten to a certain point. Finally, Chiba Sensei told her, after three years in Japan, to return to the States. He said, "Your training's not over, but it's time to start teaching. As you teach, you'll develop more concrete questions. You'll understand more what you don't know, and what you need to know. At that point, you can come back if you want with your questions."*

LORRAINE: That was the way he booted us out of the nest. That was probably more scary for me than when I went to Japan. In Japan, I was a student. I did have some responsibilities, but no heavy ones. I just did what the teacher showed, and I worked hard at it. I didn't have to think, "Will I be able to give something to each student that walks in my door? Will my students like me? Will my students want to learn from me? Will I be able to deal with it if huge guys come in to challenge me?"

I had gotten used to the way of life and the lack of violence in the country: being able to work a few hours a week, and having the rest of the time, and the money to do whatever I wanted.

My last month in Japan, I spent a lot of time sitting over coffee with Chiba Sensei talking about all my fears as a woman going back to open a school and teach in America.

He was supportive. He told me a story based upon the animal kingdom, comparing a rabbit and a tiger. At first sight, the tiger appears stronger and fiercer, easily able to defeat a rabbit. But if the rabbit uses its cunning and speed, it can survive against the tiger. Not if it goes face to face, but if it uses its abilities to its best.

He taught me I had very strong abilities, and I shouldn't compare myself to other people who I think are stronger or bigger, that

I should look at what my strengths were and develop them. Then I would have everything that I need.

He helped put my fears at rest.

Coming back here was difficult. I had been away three years. I pictured that women's rights and black civil rights must have evolved. When I got back here, everything was horrible. Women's rights hadn't gotten anywhere, and civil rights pretty much had not made any more steps.

At that time, everyone wanted to nuke the Ayatollah. I wanted to leave. I wanted to run back to Japan and hide. I thought, "I can't do this." But luckily I didn't have enough money, so I had to stay here.

She and her husband returned to the University of Massachusetts Amherst's aikido group. In 1980, they got the group committed enough to open a dojo, *which she ran with her husband.*

LORRAINE: I would never ever again run a *dojo* with a male.

ANDREA: Why?

LORRAINE: He and I were the same rank. He was very threatened by my abilities, which I never understood. I gave him credit for being bigger and stronger than I was. When people would ask me who was better, I would say he was. If people asked him, he would say he was.

I was willing to give it away. But he was very competitive. In the *dojo,* he took all the positions of responsibility and power. If we ran a test, he was the one who called the names and the techniques that people had to do. When decisions were being made, he was the one who stated what the decision was. We would talk about it, but I was kept in the background.

The students got upset with us over time. They kept saying to me, "We want you to stand up and say stuff." The problem was, if we had a disagreement in the *dojo,* I knew I was going to have to deal with that when I got home, too. It was easier for me to stay in the background and not have to deal with it later.

I had my name legally changed so that I was a distinct person from him, and the next step was the divorce. Once that happened,

I suddenly started getting a lot more credit and credence among the hierarchy of the aikido world.

I stayed and taught in the school. I maintained a back position even though I was no longer married to him. It was easier to do that. About that time, I heard Aikido of Berkeley needed an instructor. I thought, "This might be a good opportunity for me to get away, run a school on my own, see how I would do all by myself." I applied for a job, and after a lot of time and effort on their part, they hired me.

It was the best move that I had ever made. They had a hundred-member school. I was in charge of everything. I had to look at my students and see what they needed. What needed to change—what could stay the same—what needed to improve. I didn't have to go and convince someone else that it was their idea, and that it was a good idea. I made the mistakes if there were mistakes, or I made the positive gains. I liked having that responsibility. The students flourished.

Chiba Sensei, who visited the *dojo,* was incredibly supportive. He kept telling me that I'd done wonders with the group. He was thrilled, which was nice for me. And I became much more independent, and very sure of what aikido was for me, and what role I should take as a teacher.

Lorraine's students wanted her to stay, but she didn't like California. She stayed there for two-and-a-half years. She wanted to come back East. Chiba Sensei, who was then living in San Diego, was in charge of the western region of an aikido association. She talked with him, and he was supportive about her coming back. He told her she needed to open her own school.

LORRAINE: When I arrived in Berkeley, he said to me, because of the teacher-student relationship we had, "How much supervision do you want from me with your school?"

By asking me what I wanted, he put me on par with him for the first time. I said, "I want to make all my own decisions within the school. I want you to be there for me when I need you: to talk or train." We shook hands on the deal, and he never overstepped it. He let me do what I felt was right, and let it work or not work. When

I asked him for help, he was always there.

We've had our ups and downs. Our biggest down was when Paul and I got divorced. Chiba Sensei had known us as a couple. Being a Japanese male, he didn't understand divorce. He was very quick to blame the woman for not doing things right. We had no children. We'd been married twelve years so it was clearly my fault.

I went out to visit him after the divorce. It was the first time in my life that I was living alone. I had gone from my parents to college to marriage. I was having a hard time. I had to become very . . . not snooty, but self-centered. I had to really think about what I needed. It was important for me in order to survive.

He saw that and interpreted me as egotistical. I was supposed to spend two weeks training with him, and for the first time, he yelled at me for everything and anything. I left on the fifth day. I came back East. I waited a week and let my anger and hurt cool down, and then I wrote him a very long letter explaining to him what it was like for me as a woman to suddenly be on my own at thirty, to try to piece my life together and figure out who I was.

Then, we finally talked about the way he had treated me. He said, "I had not realized what you might be going through in terms of the divorce, and I will give you all the space and time you need. I hope it won't destroy our relationship as student–teacher, and I will be there for you if you need me." That felt good.

I went to a lot of counseling at that time because I almost quit aikido. I was doing aikido for Chiba Sensei's approval. I was not thinking about what aikido was for me. Like a lot of people who come up, I started to lay things on my teacher. My teacher almost in a way became a god.

The counselor I was seeing, having no idea what martial arts are, and not understanding the bond that happens between student and teacher, made me explain. In trying to explain, I started to realize what I was doing, where the problems were, and how I was asking him to be more than was fair.

I realized that he was a human being, not a god. He couldn't run my life. It was a real growth period for me, and for him, I think. It has continued. We have a strong, independent relationship now, and I like it. Things he does that I support and believe in, I'll go along with. When he oversteps and does something that I can't tolerate or support, I tell him. He listens to me and accepts what I have to say. Sometimes he's even changed what he's done, saying, "Oh, you made me think. I think you're right. I'm going to change. I won't do that."

It's been a much more rich, rewarding relationship than I think it would have been had we not gone through that falling-out time.

ANDREA: As a teacher, how do you keep an appropriate distance from the students who want to make a hero out of you?

LORRAINE: I noticed that Chiba Sensei would very willingly get involved in the students' personal lives. When a student would come with personal problems—I think that was one of the ways he allowed them to keep him in that godlike thing—he started helping them, directing their lives, and telling them what to do.

My students come to me with the same things. I let them talk, and I listen. I tell them very clearly, "I will not tell you what to do. I will listen. I will try to show you where maybe you lost logic and are not following a logical pattern, or what I see in you about what's happening, and make you question and deal with it yourself. I won't run your life. I won't make decisions."

Students ask, "Should I go to San Diego and study with Chiba Sensei?"

I throw the question back, "Do you want to?"

They say, "Yes."

I ask, "Why do you want to?" I make them start examining and deciding on their own. I say, "Whatever your decision is, I'll support you."

I try to be friendly with my students, but yet not so friendly that I lose the line of respect. I used to puzzle over it all the time, trying to figure out what I needed to do. One day, I said, "I'm not going to think about it. I'm going to be myself and see what happens."

I can't be real severe and angry on the mat as a method of teaching. I'm very lighthearted. I joke. I make my students laugh when they see their mistakes. I feel they learn better under that circumstance. But I make it very clear that if they step over a certain line, I'm not going to be laughing. I'm going to be angry.

It works well. My students listen. They work hard. Every now and then, I get mad at them, but their reaction when I get a little bit mad tells me that I've hit the line right. Everyone straightens up. They prefer me in the other mode. If I was angry and yelling and severe and stern all the time, how would I show them when I was displeased?

ANDREA: When you almost quit aikido, why did you stay?

LORRAINE: I realized that just going out on the mat each day and practicing was important for me. I couldn't walk away from it. When I did, it didn't feel like there was a central force in my life. There was nothing to really hold me together.

I also felt that through all my study, teachers had given 150% of themselves to me, and I owed the aikido world a lot. My way of repaying that was to teach. I said, "OK. Let me buckle down and get myself together. I'm not going to quit. That's running away. I'm going to dedicate myself to this and work through it."

Teaching is an incredible experience. It doesn't matter what mood I'm in when I get there. As soon as I start teaching, I am so happy. When students understand, make a breakthrough, or get excited about something they've done, I feel good. It's a feeling that can't be matched in any other way. I don't care about money or anything but just being there.

I teach a class, and I think, "It was a pretty boring class. I didn't do much."

Then, students come up to me and say, "That was a great class."

I think, "Were we in the same class? Obviously it didn't do anything for me, but it's done something for them. So, it's worth it."

My students learn a lot. They're happy. They love me as a teacher. That all feels good. I suppose I shouldn't examine it too much. I'll get crazy trying to find out what's good and what's bad.

When Lorraine came back from California, she decided she wanted to open a school in Springfield, which is about twenty-five miles south of where her ex-husband's school is. There was no place locally to train except for her ex-husband's dojo. *She got a lot of flak from him. It got to the point where she was so uncomfortable going there she couldn't train. She stopped regular training in aikido for about a year and a half.*

LORRAINE: I was doing it in my mind. I went to every seminar that was offered, but I didn't train on a daily basis. I did everything I could to stay as physically active as possible. And I kept adding to it. I started doing weight lifting intensely. I joined aerobics classes. It took seven or eight different activities for me to feel even close to the satisfaction that aikido gave me. I was running around like crazy picking up all these new hobbies.

I was afraid that my aikido was going to fall apart by the time that I opened the school, that it wouldn't be any good. I'd get depressed, and think, "I'll never find a space. I'll never get the money, and I won't be a teacher after all. I am going to have to get a regular job, and be a regular person."

Anyway, my parents gave me money to start the school. I had to make inroads. People were saying, "Who's your instructor going to be?"

I said, "Me."

They'd say, "No. Who's your male instructor going to be?"

Male students still come in and say, "I'd like to talk to the chief instructor."

I say, "You are."

They say, "No. I mean the man in charge of everything."

I say, "I am." Then I say, "If you really want to talk to a man, you came to the wrong place."

Or men will come in and say, "I've never learned anything from a woman. I don't think I can." Some have admitted that, joined, and now are among my best students. But others just will not break down. They say, "No. I'm not going to let a woman throw me around." And they walk out.

I thought I was going to have a predominantly female *dojo*. However, my *dojo* is less than 20 percent women. Mostly I have a lot of big, strong men who've come from other arts. I thought I would be challenged, but they come in, they watch me, and then they just want to study.

Probably my biggest worry is why I don't draw women in. Is it the climate of the country at this time? Is it me? As I talk to other people in other *dojos* around this country, it seems to be the climate. Women are leaving protection up to the men in their lives. I've heard women say: "I don't have time to worry about defending myself now."

ANDREA: What's your response to that?

LORRAINE: I find it hard to believe. There's so much violence on the street. If I respect myself, then I'm going to do whatever it takes to make sure I survive. When women say they don't have enough time to worry about it now, I say, "Well, obviously you're not important to yourself. You're letting other things be more important to you, like how much money you make. Isn't your life worth taking the time for?"

I don't wait for an answer. I let them mull it over. I hope that maybe, in the next year or so, they will decide that they are worth it.

ANDREA: What was it like to stop teaching?

LORRAINE: I felt bottled up. I felt like my mind, my body, everything was full to the brim with stuff to give out and no place to get rid of it. I was almost drowning in my own knowledge, and my need to give out information through teaching.

Finally I got my school opened. Chiba Sensei came out to run my grand opening. My aikido felt a lot more powerful and grounded. I felt like I had taken a step through into this giant new room, and I couldn't see walls or ceilings. It was like I could just go on forever in it. And I didn't understand exactly how I got there.

He watched my students, and he watched me train, and then he said to me, "That year and a half off was probably the best time that you've spent in aikido."

I said, "What do you mean?"

He said, "At your level, you needed to learn to let go of technique. You had been into such a grind of training and technique that you couldn't see beyond it."

Taking the time off was letting ego go, letting everything go. I felt that I probably was technically terrible, so I thought, "I'm terrible so let me just do what I can do." By doing that, I let my body move how it wanted to. Then my mind was free to take any leaps and bounds that it had been anxious to do. I'd been holding it back. It's like magic, but it's not.

I'd heard that O'Sensei said, "You learn technique, and then you reach a point where you forget technique."

I thought, "Why would you learn it if you're going to forget it? That's one of those things he said when he was off in nowhere land, and we don't know what he meant." But now I have an idea.

When I'm doing it right, I'm not thinking about what my feet and hands are doing. I'm feeling what happens. If the person who's attacking me does something out of the ordinary, that's fine. I wasn't expecting anything in particular. I can respond to exactly what comes. It's like starting aikido all over again.

I love going around and throwing all of my students. There was a stage when I didn't like to throw beginners. My excuse was, "They don't fall good, so I don't look good when I throw them, so I don't want to throw them. I'll throw my good students. They fly around and make me look impressive." And now I love to throw my beginning students.

I have a four- to six-year-olds class, and I love trying to do techniques on them. They have all kinds of different responses. To be able to do a technique, and feel what happens and how they respond is fun.

ANDREA: How do you teach the little ones how to be safe?

LORRAINE: I teach them stance. How to be balanced. I teach them that they have to be like a tree, and they have to form roots in the ground. I go around, and I test their roots, pushing and pulling. I make a game out of it. I teach them coordination, flexibility.

We've got set things to do, and they have to listen to me. At the end, I make them be trees. Then I say, "O.K. It's your turn. Try to knock me over." And they go wild trying to do it.

I never liked children before. I felt threatened by them. People kept calling and asking about four-year-old classes, and I thought, "You can't teach a four-year-old aikido, and I don't want to do day care." Then I thought, "Well, I could play games that make them think about their center and stuff like that."

We put on their little *gis* and their belts, and I grab their center, and I tell them, "Now what does it feel like when I pull you like this?" They have all kinds of stories about their centers, and what their center did all week.

And my seven- to twelve-year-olds are great. They learn a lot of technique. I've been teaching them *jo. Jo* is a short staff. I teach them forms that they can practice by themselves. In most cases, when the kids train at home, they go into their room, and close the door. They won't even let their parents watch. They know if they want me to teach it, they've got to keep it to themselves. I say, "If you've got friends who want to learn, you bring them here."

They become attached to me. Had this happened early in my teaching, I think I would have totally freaked out. Just not feeling that I was a strong enough person to have all these people depending on me. But now it feels good, and makes me feel that I'm doing something right. And that I can keep working at it. It can only get better.

I'm a professional. Aikido is the only job I do. It's who I am. I've been working hard in the past couple of years to be someone outside of it.

ANDREA: What other things do you do?

LORRAINE: I started bowling. I wanted to do something that took me out in the masses. I love it. They say, "You're an aikido teacher? Oh, fine." They couldn't care less. I've been having a ball with that. I got a lot of flak from my friends who thought it was weird that I would want to associate with people who bowl: like bowlers were second-class citizens.

Learning to bowl, I was listening to people who were trying to help me, telling me, "You have to move through the ball. You have to extend your power beyond . . .

And I thought, "Oh, God. I think I've heard this before. Now how do I apply it to a bowling ball?"

I got to be a beginner again. It's helpful in teaching. I'm twenty-one years into doing a martial art. It's hard for me to identify with the person who's just walked on the mat on their first day: their frustration about being a beginner and their fear of doing something wrong.

ANDREA: For the future, what do you want for yourself?

LORRAINE: I hope a woman student comes in who I can train all the way to black belt, who wants to be a teacher, and she goes on and surpasses me.

I've got a little eight-year-old student right now who tells me all the time, "I'll stay with you, and I'm going to study with you, and when you get too old to teach, I'll take over for you. I'll take care of you."

I almost cry every time she says it. It's so nice, and she's very serious. She's been with me for two years now, and her dad trains, too. She's totally committed. I hope that maybe she will be the one that stays with me all the way through.

I'd like for my school to be successful. By successful, I mean that I get a large number of students who become very committed to the way of aikido and in some way give back to the aikido community.

I'd like to be able to make a comfortable living. I'd like to not be freaking out about my bills the first of every month.

I intend to do aikido forever. I make jokes about coming on the mat with my walker. But I want it to be like that.

Carol Sanoff

CAROL SANOFF *was raised in Pennsylvania and California, and graduated from UC Berkeley with degrees in comparative literature and library science. Her principal aikido teacher has been Robert Nadeau. She lives with her husband in Sonoma County, California, and has recently left a twenty-year career working with computers in order to do body work and teach awareness and authenticity through movement.*

I drove deep into cow country to meet with Carol Sanoff. The hills were brilliant green, the Holsteins looked almost sculptural against the hillsides. Amidst the farms is the city of Santa Rosa, complete with a red brick mall, a health food store, and a few choice vintage clothing stores. From the front step of the building where I met Carol, I could see the green hills which surround the city. At the office door, she greeted me and showed me into a waiting room with calming, wheat-colored walls and a comfortable black leather couch. On the floor were neat stacks of flyers describing her form of body work, Authentic Movement, and aikido.

The office itself was large and pleasant with natural light, a body work table, couch, and shelves of books. Wooly tapestries and handmade weavings in muted hues hung on the walls.

During the interview, Carol sat curled up in a chair except when talking about her passions. Then, she would put both feet on the floor and lean forward with a gaze of great intensity.

Carol started training in aikido in 1979 while she was finishing her master's degree in library science at the University of California at Berkeley. As a child, she was a tomboy, but she didn't find a sport she excelled at until college. As an undergraduate, she was a member of the women's rowing team. After college, she made the national team twice and was on the Olympic Committee for four years.

CAROL: In a way, rowing was my first spiritual practice although I didn't know it then. It was certainly my first body practice.

Rowing was a wonderful part of my life. I loved the intensity of training. I loved racing less because the added intensity was almost too much for me. When I decided to stop training, I was twenty-six years old and thought I was old. I could also see—I'm not very big—that the next wave of rowers would be a lot faster than I was. At that point, I was as good as I was going to get. I also wanted something more.

I was beginning to get information from my rowing training. Insights would come into my mind and I didn't know how I knew these things. I'd be running, having decided ahead of time I would run three miles, would get to three miles and not be tired. What were these limits that I set up? I was learning things about myself that were important. I wanted more of that kind of insight.

I was tired of the actual physical training. From rowing I went to folk dancing and then to t'ai chi, but I was floating without an intense attachment to anything. I'd heard of aikido, and one day I decided to go watch an aikido class. I looked in the phone book, and found Aikido of San Francisco. When I went to the *dojo* after work, I watched a class taught by a teacher who was vivid and alive, asking questions of the room in general that nobody'd ever asked me, but questions I wanted to be asked.

Like: "Why are you apologizing for being here?" I realized I'd been apologizing all my life. He was asking about who I was, and asking me to be more. I was immediately hooked.

Aikido itself looked very strange to me, not at all like t'ai chi. I thought, "He's asking good questions, so I'll come and train. But I don't know whether I can roll and fall like that." And I didn't at first. I was really afraid for a long time. (I got by that one day when another teacher of mine picked me up and threw me. I was in the air, and then I was on the mat, and I was still intact. When I realized I'd survived, I wanted to try it again.)

I had thought I would travel after I finished my master's degree. And I didn't. By the time I left the *dojo* that day, I knew I wasn't going anywhere.

She started training. She went to all of her teacher's noon classes and evening classes. For several years, aikido became her focus of attention. She found a mostly-weekend job as a cook and had time to do a lot of aikido.

ANDREA: When your teacher asked the "right questions," what did you find in yourself?

CAROL: I found space, more joy, intense fear, and a fierce will to excel. There's a lot of joy on the mat. I tend to be melancholy and to contain my excitement and joy: I think I learned as a child to hide these parts of myself, not trusting how the adults around me would respond.

The practice of aikido seems to invite the exploration of power, so I felt safe to express my exuberance, my excitement, and my pleasure on the mat.

ANDREA: Did your family have a reaction to you doing a martial art?

CAROL: When I was rowing, my mother used to look at my hands and say, "Nobody's ever going to marry you with hands like that." Because of my difficulties with my mother I was always doing my life a little bit differently. My mother would say to me, "You shouldn't beat the boys at tennis." I would beat them if I could. I didn't care about that kind of socialization.

Neither of my parents have ever seen me do aikido. My guess is that they might see the form differently than I experience it.

ANDREA: Did the black belt have meaning for you when you began to train?

CAROL: Not really. I had just finished this master's program and jumped through a bunch of somebody else's hoops. I was not interested in belts and did not take any belt tests.

ANDREA: Ever?

CAROL: Until I took my black belt test.

ANDREA: That's it?

CAROL: That's it. It was very arrogant of me. I wouldn't suggest other people do it. But I wasn't there for belts. I was there to learn some things. Also I'm not very good at performance.

When it seemed to be time for me to think about doing a black belt test, it was hard for me. I didn't have a graceful way to move into it, and I hadn't practiced taking tests. I took a fairly awful test, relative to the aikido I was able to do.

For my ongoing training, I was there as much as I could be. I knew something important would happen if I went to class, and it almost always did. I didn't say to myself: "I think I'll go today" or "I don't think I'll go today." I just went. I trained as hard as I could.

What could have been added by my being interested in the belts? Maybe some refinement of technique; but my instructor was teaching about energy, about being bigger, having power, and staying connected to the ground. It didn't matter what the technique was, who I was training with, or what rank I was.

But after several years, I wanted to join the big kids. It seemed like it was time. And we had moved up here to Santa Rosa, away from the *dojo* where I was training. For awhile, I was commuting to the city to work. But when my job and commute changed, I knew that my training in the city was going to decrease and that if I was going to take a black belt test, I needed to do it.

My aikido got awful. I was trying to learn all the techniques I hadn't paid sufficient attention to because I was more interested in energy. People were shouting at me to bend my knees, and find my knees. I thought I knew what my knees were doing and apparently I didn't.

It was a pretty uncomfortable time—I wondered if I was going to be able to do a good enough job. After the test I felt free. It was just wonderful. I could go back and just train. I could go be a white belt again if I wanted to be. I didn't have to try to do "good, succinct technique."

ANDREA: What do you like best about training?

CAROL: The contact and the play, the intimacy. For me, something of me began to emerge, "Oh there's somebody in here, actually!" I was in my mid-thirties, and a very late bloomer. Maybe that's partly a gift, too, but it's also painful: I didn't know who I was for the longest time. I didn't even know enough to ask questions. But once I started asking, I was free to find all kinds of possible answers.

Also, during training, you get what's essential about a person, because you don't exchange your life histories, you just start training together. Soon you know, "This person's a little stiff in the shoulder. This person will meet my gaze. This person will play with me. This person won't play with me. This person wants to be a little apart from me. Or a little better than me. This one wants me to be the expert." You know about the person before you know the social things that we generally know about people.

Despite what we think, that there are secrets about us that nobody knows, it's pretty clear on the mat who we really are, for anybody with eyes to see that. And it's quite wonderful actually to be able to touch each other. That's a real gift of aikido. I often think of puppies in a litter and how we get to go back and do that. A lot of times when I'm warming my class up, I'll try to get them to giggle, be silly, or flop around a little bit so it's not too serious. Part of the joy of it is just being able to be childlike and unsophisticated with each other, touching and holding and all that stuff. Not only do we have to do it because that's how we do aikido, but we get to enjoy it as well.

ANDREA: When I think of intimacy, I think of sexuality, which is different from what you're talking about.

CAROL: I think they are different, and I think they can occur together. It's the same kind of intimacy as being able to sit with a friend, and look at them, and not say anything for a while; or sit with somebody who's very sad, and just be there with them.

ANDREA: Was there anything you hated about training?

CAROL: One of my teachers had an uncanny ability to find my weakest place and not let go. The unremitting attention on parts of me that probably were never going to get very good—and certainly weren't very good at the moment—was very painful. Although that feedback was very important to me, at times when my ego was pretty wobbly, it got flattened by that information.

And sometimes when I teach I feel totally inadequate. When I teach classes lately, I find I'm not so interested in technique, even though it gives me a frame to work with. I'm interested in: "Are people willing to touch and be touched? What's the quality of the contact? Can we do a technique and have eye contact, or do we have to put up barriers? Is it possible to do a task and also be in kind of a living, liquid, moving edge of contact with somebody?" That kind of contact translates to other life situations. Life gets dead and dull when I've got walls up that say, "No, you can't feel through here, you have to put your feelings on this side. I'll keep my feelings on the other side. We're not allowed to make contact." We become isolated from each other and from ourselves too.

Aikido is valuable to see how alive I am—or how alive I'm not—in a context which is safe and encourages inquiry. It gives me options for being more wild, crazy, sensitive, quiet, whatever, in other parts of my life.

Probably everybody has had the experience of somebody really listening to them, and felt how that has changed them. In aikido there's something about stilling all the busyness, all the need to be better than, or need to be good enough (the possibilities of real stillness, which I learned first in t'ai chi), that leaves me free and gives me more options.

ANDREA: Can you give an example of how you would use aikido in a personal relationship?

CAROL: It has been hardest for me to take aikido principles into my closest relationships, because they're the ones that really matter, where I'm afraid to be powerful and pushy, where the weird and vulnerable parts of me are most likely to surface, and where I feel least skilled. My experience when I'm out of alignment with myself is one of internal discomfort. I get anxious. My husband might say to me that my face is all twisted up. I wasn't aware of feeling that. It's very painful both to feel that I'm anxious and to feel how far from myself I've been.

It shifts either when I get so clear about it that I know what's going on, or I get so uncomfortable I can't stand it anymore. I want to go in there, go where that discomfort is. And simultaneously I want to get as far away from it as I can.

When I'm working well I try to think of one true thing I could say. I start with that. I try not only to say it, but to stay there with it. Instead of lobbing it out and staying back here, I take one step forward truly.

ANDREA: Is it like *ukemi*, the attack, in aikido?

CAROL: In the same way that *ukemi* is a foolish thing to do because you know you're going to take a fall. I always feel, "Well, no ego is going to be preserved here, but something has to move, so I'm going to take a step forward, and see what will happen." It's a kind of sacrifice.

In the case of relationship difficulties, it feels like sacrifice of somebody I'd like to get rid of and I can't—a part of me that learned to cope in various neurotic ways with the world. In a way it's not a sacrifice but it's awfully scary sometimes to say, "I'm pissed off and I'm not feeling like it's OK to say that." Having said that, there's no clear resolution. That's the next, most immediate step, but I don't know where it goes from there. I have to get there and then figure out what to do. Maybe there isn't any place close, and I have to hang out for awhile.

In 1986, after doing some substitute teaching, Carol accepted Bob Noha's offer to teach a weekly class at his dojo in Petaluma.

CAROL: It's an honor to teach, and it's also very humbling. It feels like the practice of teaching is to stay in the body, stay aware, stay with my own questions, and bring all of that with me onto the mat.

Teaching for Bob is a wonderful situation, because the people are already there, they love aikido, and they love Noha. I couldn't have asked for more ideal circumstances to learn how to teach. I still fumble a lot. My students will laugh at me, and I laugh with them.

ANDREA: At the time, how did it feel to stop being the student and start being the teacher?

CAROL: Actually, I don't think I've ever stopped being a student; I still train. In aikido, the second day you're on the mat, you know something more than a person who just got on the mat for the first time. As you train with people you're always teaching one another.

The weight of learning shifts around so that becoming a teacher in front of the class is a more formalized version. It is an exchange: "Could we slow down? How do I do this? Could you try that?"

ANDREA: What is the essence of the student-teacher relationship?

CAROL: I think it is about longing and love. We are longing, as students, to become more of ourselves. And love is the medium that allows us to grow. That's oversimplified, obviously, and probably quite personal. For myself, I usually feel something like love for my significant teachers, and that keeps my attention focused, keeps me coming back for more. And as I keep coming back, they can teach me.

I remember sitting with someone watching a class at an aikido retreat. The students were bowing to a teacher. While the teacher bowed back to them, they all kept their foreheads down to the mat, the way they do in some classes. I said to my friend, "It looks like groveling to me." I prefer that the students be upright and full, and have some kind of integrity and balance about themselves. What the teacher does is offer. What the student does is accept or not.

When I was newly teaching, I struggled a lot. Another neophyte teacher said to me, "When I teach I just think of myself as the guy with the key to the *dojo* whose turn it is to say, 'Let's do this.' And we all do this."

But what's also true is that a teacher has been down the path already, and knows it fairly well. A teacher gets to use his eyes and experience to help. Teachers can be wrong. And students know a lot, before they even begin aikido. A teacher needs to respect that.

ANDREA: I'm grateful when my aikido teacher screws up, because I get to see she's human. I have a tendency to want to deify.

CAROL: You give your power away when you do that.

ANDREA: Power can't be "given away." That phrase doesn't sit right with me.

CAROL: Perhaps not. But you can stop being your own authority, in response to thinking somebody else knows more. You can listen more to somebody else than you do to yourself for a period of time.

I try to listen from my heart and my longing to be who I need to be. I listen for clues, resonances, and truth.

ANDREA: I love the gear. I love putting on the funny suit. What is it like for you?

CAROL: I like my *gi* better as it's gotten soft and frayed and old-looking. I love the *hakama*—this long black skirt-like thing that I get to wear, which touches the ground and moves beautifully.

A friend saw me in training garb recently for the first time. She works in a hospital, and I had gone by to drop some cookies off on my way to teach. She had known that I did aikido, and she said later, "I understood something about your martial art, when I saw how you were dressed." Something happened for her, seeing the outfit.

ANDREA: Anything else about the gear?

CAROL: I've never been really good at weapons, but I like the beauty and the simplicity of them. I regret that weapons are not part of my expertise because there's something about the sword work in aikido that is quite lovely.

ANDREA: How would you compare doing body work to doing aikido?

CAROL: Both are about contact, aliveness, balance, and boundaries. The forms are different but the intention in both is to learn and be more of who we are.

We get to say, in aikido and in body work, "This time together is important. Let's be here as fully as we can. Maybe this relates to the rest of our lives or maybe it doesn't, but let's allow ourselves to take being here seriously."

One way this became clear to me was when a friend of mine died suddenly. It made me look at my other relationships and ask, "Is this my last opportunity to be with this person? Am I saying what is true and important to say, or am I acting in a habitual way?"

Also, we train with people over time, and see them change. And we have this agreement with one other that the *dojo* is a place where we're going to work together. We're not here to bullshit each other or break bones. We're here to work on ourselves and see how clear we can get.

Someone in my class right now is taking a long time off because of a sore back. He hates to miss any training, but he's learned that when he's ready to come back, the *dojo* will be there. The *dojo* endures over time—we can keep coming to it and keep coming to ourselves in it.

My teacher, Robert Nadeau, has tremendous charisma and tremendous passion about his aikido. When I have tried to teach classes like his, they have never worked. But sometimes I find my own love and passion and teach from that. There are times when I go to class and think, "Somebody else should be teaching tonight. I don't know very much." That's not comfortable. But there are times when I go, and I know why I love it.

It feels like students see light in their teachers, and find a similar light in themselves. They begin to find ways to feed their own light.

I don't do much: I hold the door open so people can be what they want to be. I can't light a fire, if it's not already there. I can offer somebody encouragement, but people teach themselves, and I give them a space where they can do it. I give them as much love and attention as I can, and try to remind myself and them to be patient. Some alchemy happens.

ANDREA: This is paradoxical: a martial art enabling these kinds of things to happen. Did you expect this?

CAROL: I didn't come in looking for a self-defense art. I was looking for myself. The essence of any kind of self-defense is awareness. If you're not aware of danger, you can't move. Looking at awareness from an aikido perspective, I became interested in asking, "What is it about me that's not comfortable? What is it about me that gets pissed off? Why am I not OK with myself?"

The things that look magical to a new student, can look less so with more experience. After a while you think, "Well, I could do that. I know that one." But there are people who still look quite magical to me in their aikido. Either they're particularly clean about their technique or there's a particular presence about them.

ANDREA: Is there a danger in having that presence?

CAROL: There can be. Just as in any art, people get good at aikido. Maybe being good takes them a little bit away from the primary practice of exploration or growth. It is typical that when people get to the brown belt level, they want to know "if this stuff really works." They start testing their power and seeing if their training partners are really affected. It's a detour. I guess it's only dangerous if they don't come back again. One definition of a "journey" is to travel somewhere and then return changed by the experience. It's fine to work with power as long as we don't lose our connection, humility, and the simple practice of being present.

When I talk about the simple practice, what I mean is, a lot of people walk around knowing they have a body but not really inhabiting it, in a detailed, specific, or kinesthetic way. The clearer I am about being embodied, the more possibilities there are for being alive. That's a crucial component to aliveness, which has to do with vibrancy and growth. The body is the foundation for the real, tender leaves of who I am, not yet, but who I could be, blooming or growing.

Centeredness doesn't come from anywhere. We just finally find it, I think. Centeredness is already there, and we finally quiet down enough and focus so that we are there in alignment with it.

Grounding is a practice of coming back to experiencing the body again and again, such that it becomes almost a constant, a place to work from rather than, "something to get back to once in a while when I remember." Once it's there as a place to work from, we can go on to whatever that wants to support. It can be any number of things.

There are people who know this intuitively. Before aikido, I was fairly embodied but not so aware. I had to bring my awareness back.

ANDREA: Could you describe the differences between who you were and what you are like now?

CAROL: Well, I'm still shy and frightened and clumsy at times, but a little more aware of my "stuff" and a little more willing to take interpersonal risks. We don't know how it is that we change and grow, really, but I think the practice of aikido and ongoing participation in the aikido community have been very beneficial for me.

People look more and more like themselves as they do aikido. I don't think they look more like their teacher or more like a martial artist.

ANDREA: What lessons remain for you in aikido?

CAROL: Probably all of them. Less fear and self-absorption, more courage, risk-taking, play. The frontiers of pleasure and joy seem to want exploration. There are skills and techniques that need work and polish, and it seems that as I work on myself, my aikido changes.

ANDREA: What other things have your passion?

CAROL: What's common to the things that I feel passionate about is that they take me toward the true and the luminous. Vipassana meditation (both daily practice and occasional retreats) is fundamental to my life.

I also practice a discipline called Authentic Movement which is a very open exploration of self and awareness through movement.

There's nothing I love better than being deeply touched—it can be by a person, a letter, a sunset. It's a privilege to be here, alive on this planet, and I want to stay awake for it as much as possible. When you ask about passion, the focus for me is: how alive can I be in ordinary circumstances, in the grocery store line, which is one of my worst places? I get bitchy in the grocery store line. I think, "Would you guys please... Ten items, the sign says." Why not be full and alive there too? It's certainly not a passionate place for me, but why not?

I would like not to resist my life. In the grocery line, I think: "I don't want to be here. Please get out of my way."

ANDREA: I'm good at being here now when it's ecstasy, but . . .

CAROL: . . . when it's boring . . .

ANDREA: . . . when I haven't done my dishes for a week, I don't want to be there now. Despite the fact that it's the thing to do.

ANDREA: Have you ever had to use your martial arts skill?

CAROL: After I'd been practicing about a year and a half, I parked one evening in a very bad part of San Francisco. I walked to the *dojo*, took a class, and walked, schlepping my purse and *gi* bag, back to my car. I'd put the key in my car door, when I heard footsteps behind me. I turned around, and a man was running across the street. I thought, "Oh, isn't that interesting." Then, I realized he was running at me. I thought, "Oh, jeez." He grabbed my purse, and I grabbed my purse, because what went through my mind was, "If he gets my purse he's going to know where I live, and I don't want him to know that."

I was also afraid he might have a weapon but I didn't want to let go of my purse. So we circled around it like two dogs around a bone. At some point, he dropped it and ran back across the street. At this point, I realized I'd been screaming the whole time. Some people had come out of a fire station at the other end of the block, because I'd been screaming.

I would say that my aikido training pretty much left me, except that I stayed grounded in the tussle over the purse.

ANDREA: Do you feel safe in the world, or different than you did in the world before you started?

CAROL: I am more awake, and so probably more aware of feeling safe and of not feeling safe. I feel my life belongs to me. I'm less and less able to try to figure out from what somebody else says what I really should be doing. As far as I get in life, I have myself to thank or blame, not somebody else.

ANDREA: What would you say to a person who wants to try aikido?

CAROL: Find a class to watch. And if you get drawn into it, find a teacher and a *dojo* that feel right. Spend some time with it, and take it slowly. Enjoy the process of learning and of being a beginner. It's a long path and once you start you'll probably be on it for some time, so don't rush yourself.

Cress Forester

Let the beauty you love be what you do.
There are thousands of ways to kneel and kiss the ground.
—Jelaluddin Rumi (1207–1273 A.D.),
    as heard on Cress's answering machine message.

Born in London, England, in 1954, CRESS FORESTER *has a B.A. in politics and economics from Leeds University in England. She studied law at Leeds Polytechnic and counselling at San Francisco State University and the Professional School of Psychology in San Francisco. She has also studied CranioSacral Therapy, Ortho-Bionomy, Body-Mind Centering, and Continuum Dance-Voice Meditation. She currently has a private practice as a bodytherapist in San Francisco.*

Cress has taken a radical position in relationship to aikido: she refuses to work with strikes or blows any longer because she is not willing to contribute toward the violence in the world. At the time I interviewed her, she had stopped wearing her black belt and hakama when she taught or practiced aikido, and would wear her gi and white belt instead.

Cress met me at the front door of her building, perched on a hill overlooking the San Francisco Bay. Before I entered her apartment, I slipped off my shoes and placed them beside the other neatly grouped footwear outside her front door. During our interview we sat in her work room, I on a corduroy-covered futon couch, she on a window seat. After an hour or so, the rain started coming down in diagonal thin grey stripes against the window behind her. She moved in her seat as she spoke, sometimes clasping her knee, sometimes placing both feet on the ground; a few times making quota-

56

tion marks with her fingers to show the irony she was implying in her speech.

Cress came to the United States in 1979, when she fell in love with an American woman. She stayed to maintain personal freedom: "the distance from my family that I needed, and environments tremendously supportive to me as a woman, a lesbian, and a New Age health practitioner. I needed that. I needed a lot of support around all of those things, and I get it here." She started studying aikido in 1983 when she was working toward a masters in counseling at San Francisco state. In her private practice as a body-therapist, she integrates noninvasive hands-on approaches, with counselling, movement, and roleplay. She also offers classes and workshops using body awareness and movement to explore the meaning, and living, of "right relationship."

ANDREA: What was your early experience of studying aikido?

CRESS: From the moment I walked onto the mat, a voice in me said, "This will be part of your way." It was very clear. I became disenchanted with my studies, and as I dropped academic classes, I added aikido classes until I was training every day. Then, I was training two or three times a day. I was always staying after class and training with people as well. It became my life.

I became enchanted with the form and movement of it, the feeling in my body. I was hungry for the spiritual side of it: how we relate to one another, to ourselves, and to the world as beings with a God spark, or whatever language you use for that. I'm in my spiritual nature when I allow myself to feel, breathe, and act with knowledge of my own connectedness. What I have that's "spiritual" isn't only mine, it's a piece of something that we all share.

In my aikido training, what made me aware of that was some of my teachers had incredible *ki*. I felt this energy emanated from them. And that I had it, too.

In the beginning, it was infuriating. Someone said, "Feel this." And I thought, "What do you mean this? Show it to me." I looked for it with senses that don't know how to perceive it. As I developed, it became obvious, and I could say, "This stream of energy is totally clear to me. I can see how far it goes, and there's a little kink in your elbow where it's getting a little blocked." We perceive *ki* with *different* senses.

When it hooked up, it was incredible to feel my energy and theirs. From that, I eventually began to feel hooked up to a larger field of energy. In the beginning, I felt the field of it, the direction of it, and almost the compulsion of it. I felt "power" in a neutral sense: the gravitational power of it, sensing the direction my partner was coming from, and also who they were.

There were endless lessons of feeling frustrated that my partner wasn't falling or throwing me the right way, and I constantly came back to, "This is them. This is me. If they're not falling the right way, it doesn't mean that they're wrong or that I'm wrong. It just means that we're not hooked up in a way that's going to be helpful." That gave me a sense of distance from that intense engagement of acting in conflict.

ANDREA: What the Japanese call *"ma-ai"*?

CRESS: No. *Ma-ai*, as I understand it, contributes to a sense of conflict by saying, "This is my enemy, and I have to find a safe distance."

On some level the safest distance is to have no experience of distance, to see that we are one. O'Sensei wrote, "When you become the center of the universe, there's no conflict there."

When I feel I need to have some distance from you, that tells me there's something in my universe I'm not comfortable with, and that I need to create some artificial sense of distance from.

ANDREA: Was testing and belts important to you?

CRESS: It didn't seem to be until around the time I felt I was ready for my brown belt test. I had studied with many teachers from early on in my training and I started to get feedback; some of my teachers, ranked as highly, or higher than my *sensei* were saying, "Why aren't you going for the brown belt? You're ready." I would ask my *sensei,* and she'd say, "No. You need to wait." I became angry and frustrated and felt manipulated. I felt that my teacher didn't want me to be advancing as rapidly as I was. I didn't find that she gave

me appropriate answers when I would ask, "Why do you think I have to wait? These other people are saying I should have already taken it." That was very hard.

I finally took my brown belt test with that *sensei*, and then decided to leave her *dojo*. Taking my black belt test was very important to me, as a claiming of aikido and of myself, for myself.

In the beginning, I did what I was told to do in aikido. I totally surrendered to my teacher, and did what she told me to do. I wanted to learn. She was an amazing teacher of technique, and an amazingly graceful aikidoist. I was fascinated by her. I was attracted to her, and embarrassed by that.

I didn't know what to do with these feelings, and didn't do anything with them. I did say, "I just need to say I'm attracted to you. I don't need to do anything about it, but I just need to get it out because I'm so aware of it."

She didn't say anything at all. Nothing ever happened. Thank God. I didn't want anything to happen, but I did need to unburden myself. But, as her student, I handed over my power to her. I'm furious with myself. I'd like to be furious at her, but I know that the anger needs to stay with me.

I'm angry with her because she abused her power by holding me back from my test. And...she's human. She gets to do her own thing.

Around the time I came to an awakening about *my* role with her, I asked to be treated as an equal, and came to believe that she could never treat me as an equal.

I left. Since then, I have gotten a lot more perspective on my part in this. Give me an authority figure and I will either rebel or give my power to them. As I learn to catch that, I learn not to. But it's a gradual process.

ANDREA: Where did you get the presence of mind to leave?

CRESS: I was furious. Anger is always a great nudge for me. I had always trained at her *dojo,* and at another *dojo* so I was aware of another option. But hers had been my home *dojo.* I was very attached.

It felt more and more like a bad home for me. I was teacher's pet for a long time, which alienated me from the other students who resented me. I didn't see that I was teacher's pet, or my role in it. As I came to see it, I said, "I don't want to be the person who you demonstrate techniques with all the time. This doesn't feel good to me. Please choose other people." When I'd talk to my therapist about my struggles in the *dojo,* she pointed out that I had options. She would say, "Is there another place you could train?"

I would say, "Yes."

"Why don't you just train there?"

It was mind-boggling and empowering to say to myself, "This isn't working for me. At a certain point, if I can't get what I need here, I need to leave this *dojo* because this is unhealthy for me. I can get what I need elsewhere."

ANDREA: At your black belt test, what did they want to see? What did you want to show?

CRESS: I thought they wanted a level of proficiency in form and technique. Technique seemed to come easily to me. I wanted to show in my test how I could be loving to others. Of course, I utterly failed in that; I became quite flustered and panicked, and ended up throwing people around. Nevertheless, my intention was there. I never wanted to take aikido as a *martial* art. Although, once I started training, I discovered I had an incredible warrior spirit in me.

ANDREA: What does the term "woman warrior" mean to you?

CRESS: The last thing we need right now is warriors. "Spiritual warrior" is a contradiction in terms. What people are trying to reach for is the essence of a certain kind of commitment, presence, and perseverance in the face of hardship. So let's talk about that. Let's not talk about "warrior."

I was with a friend at the marina. We were talking, and a guy sat down fairly near us, close enough so that he was intruding. He had obviously been drinking. He was still drinking. He was listening in and periodically making lewd comments.

We were both aware of him being there, but we didn't address ourselves to him. Now and again my friend would look over, and check out what was going on. I was seated with my back toward him.

As we left, he came up to us and started talking nonsense. He was really saying, "You two are rich white girls, and you've got a car. And I don't." His words weren't logically that. But that was his message. And he kept talking at us. But he was talking mostly to my friend.

She looked at him and said, "Who listens to you? Whoever listens to you? This isn't a conversation. What do you want to say here?" She completely aligned herself with him, and listened to him. I watched as this man's disturbed, drunken face lightened and became transformed into an almost boyish, joyous grin.

They looked at one another for several minutes. At the end, he reached out, and they shook hands and touched shoulders. I was ashamed that I, a black belt, had been thinking about how I could physically defend my friend who is only fifth *kyu*. I want to be able to do what she did. I don't want this physical stuff, which just encourages me to think in terms of violence and force. I want to find a different form.

What else do we need to say about war? I'm not interested in it. "Woman warrior" is not a term that I like. I'm deeply skeptical about whether that path is what it claims to be.

I do have a tremendous fighting spirit. I can roust with the best of them. And I sometimes enjoy fighting—testing my strength against another's. In this sense, I'm a warrior. That's not a side of myself that I choose to develop any longer. On one level, when I'm on the mat and I throw someone, I still get a rush from it. That tells me that I'm still not at peace with something. If I still believe that this person could do some harm to me, I'm giving away my power.

I'm buying into the essence of the patriarchal conflict model, which is, "I prove that I'm worth something by beating you," rather than by having inherent virtues which don't make anyone else less.

ANDREA: From your perspective, hierarchy doesn't exist?

CRESS: When I stay in this heart place, I can feel that we all have a piece to play here. When I stay with my process long enough, I can feel that what's going on has to do with how I value myself, how I relate to myself.

ANDREA: What about the notion talked about in aikido of perceiving attacks as "gifts of energy" rather than as acts of violence?

CRESS: I worked with that for a long time. On some level, I was aware that striking another never felt good to me. Now I won't do it.

In the context of this world—where the conflict model is so embedded we don't realize it is only a model—it's a seductive and destructive lie to say that fighting is a gift of energy. The form and the intent is a strike: an invasion, a crossing of somebody's boundary, and a devaluing of their personhood, their sacredness. I don't buy that lie.

The last time I worked with strikes in an aikido class, the practice was to make contact—punch the belly. I didn't mind receiving the strike, although I felt emotionally hurt that someone would want to do this to me.

When my turn came to strike my partner, I experienced revulsion, grief, and incomprehension. I thought, "Why would I want to do this?" But, this was the practice, so I stayed with it. After awhile, I realized I was perfectly fine. I was on the line giving straight, clear energy.

I thought, "Wait a second. What's going on here?" I realized I had just blanked out whole realms of my consciousness. "This is a human being! I want to see how I'm affecting her. I don't want to needlessly cause her harm." And then I rationalized, "Well, I'm helping her learn how to deal with something like this. I value empowering and helping women learn how to protect themselves and deal with attacks."

I can't use those words to fool myself any longer. I know there are other ways of learning how to become a strong person that don't involve being violated or violating others in the process. And if I don't have to repeat abuse, I'm not going to. I search with all of my might to find alternatives. And I'm finding them.

I got distracted along that path. I believed if I trained hard and long enough, if I was sincere enough, I'd be able to handle any attack. All I did was learn to become a good fighter. Good fighters encourage other fighters to come up to them.

What about a situation where I might need to use my martial arts skills? If I'm going downtown to a demonstration, and I know that the attack squads are going to be out with their truncheons, it might be a good idea to know what to do in the face of a truncheon.

But there's a level of self-preservation, safety-creating, and peace-making that says, "Yes, they have clubs. And I want to hold this nonviolent quality so strongly that they're not going to use them." I don't want to set up an expectation: imagining the strike coming from a certain angle, so I'll move like that.

When someone attacks you, they expect you to retaliate by trying to attack and destroy them. If you make it apparent in your words and actions that you hold them in high esteem, something happens in them. They question what they're really doing, and that changes everything. Barbara Deming lived and wrote about this way of being and working for change.

The activist Barbara Deming described feeling an almost magical sense when she could utterly hold to her values. She was in very tense situations during the civil rights marches. She said sometimes she felt almost magically protected when she could sustain a perspective of nonviolent loving: "One hand gently taking away what is not theirs and the other gently calming them."

In the same way she did then, I work now with myself to find a way of standing up for myself that doesn't involve fighting. As soon as I'm fighting somebody else, I've already lost. What I need to develop is my loving compassion. Can I believe in and stand up for myself in a nonviolent, active way that honors other people? Can I say "I disagree with you" or, "That's not my perspective," without saying, "You're wrong, you're bad"?

Standing up for myself is an issue that comes up in my personal life as well. If my lover doesn't want to be with me, I can think, "Oh, she's rejecting me because I'm a bad person." Then, I think, "Wait. This is my own attack. This is my own war going on inside, saying I am a bad person." She might be saying, "You are a bad person. I don't want to be with you because you are a jerk." If I believe that, I'm in trouble. If I don't believe it, I may be hurt by her saying a hurtful thing to me, but it's on a different level than if *I* believe I'm of no worth.

Or I can think, "Oh, she doesn't want to be with me right now. She has other things to do. I'm still a worthwhile person." All this occurs in the scenario of my lover being who she is, a loving person.

ANDREA: Has being a lesbian informed your practice?

CRESS: As a lesbian, with my own internalized homophobia, and my awareness of other's homophobia, I have sometimes felt I had to keep myself apart from other women, in case they would think I was coming on to them. My fear of being accused of sexual harassment has made it harder for me to reach out.

Sometimes I've felt women shrink away when they found out I'm lesbian. In general, in aikido, I found women comfortable with me.

I've encountered homophobic comments from men in the *dojo*, which for the most part, I've let run off me. I've told myself that they didn't affect me when they did. For the most part, I have found men to be enormously friendly and warm towards me, and I haven't hidden my lesbianism.

Being physical with people was always a great challenge to me. In aikido, you were supposed to get close and roll around on the ground. It was license to be able to touch people. For the first three-and-a-half years of my aikido practice, I would greet people by going, "Hi-Ya!" and making some chop gesture. This was my way to connect with other people. These were my "social skills."

Since then, I've learned social skills. When I like seeing somebody, I can be straightforward about it, and say, "I'm glad to see you." Now I'm able to shake hands or hug people like any other human being. Aikido's such a male-dominated activity, and in some ways, male-focused activity, that, to be a woman there is to stand out. Some people think that any woman who'd do that would be a lesbian, "What are you doing aikido for unless you're a lesbian? What decent woman would do that kind of thing?"

Of course, that's nonsense.

ANDREA: A homophobic attitude seems contrary to the spirit of aikido. Do you see other unhealthy contradictions in aikido?

CRESS: O'Sensei talked about making the whole world one family. You don't pin people in a healthy family. You don't throw them away. When you have a conflict, you talk it through. You listen to one another, and you have faith that you're not enemies, that you're both loving and caring. You work it out until it's sorted out. Maybe you take time out or agree to not see each other for awhile, at the most extreme.

How are we going to learn to *work together?* I say, "I want to build a house. I want to build a co-op. I want to make a family. Will you help me?" and you say, "Yes." There's no model for that in the *forms* of aikido.

ANDREA: So, what motivates you to go on?

CRESS: My curiosity, my spirit drives me. It's being-in-the-moment-ness, a sense that immanence infuses all things. In terms of philosophy, I have always been drawn to mystical things and had a sense of the numinous.

ANDREA: What are the dangers of this?

CRESS: As a teenager, I became tremendously drawn to spiritual things and powers. Then I would stop studying and reading, because I would fear abusing these powers: that if I didn't know what I was doing, I would hurt people with it. This would keep me from pursuing metaphysical studies. I still feel that this realm is seductive. It's the realm of power.

When I'm feeling insecure—perhaps because my teaching job at the local university has been cut—I react by thinking, "Have I anything valuable to offer? Will I make my rent?" To feel secure I can think, "I'm strong. I can get on the mat and I can flip somebody. I'm skilled in this *ki* thing. I am psychic. I can read what's going on with someone." When I do it to meet some inner hunger or insecurity, it becomes risky for me.

I don't think I'm so drawn to power that I would go charging off down some manic abuse route. We are all powerful beings. The trouble occurs when we start to get a sense of what our powers are, but we still have fear running us.

I also believe there's some kind of weird pattern. Things move the way they can to try and help things play out. I can remember a day I was feeling totally powerless and dejected. I was walking down the street, it was fall, and my eye was caught by a leaf that had turned color. It was the most gorgeous chestnut brown. As I looked at it, my eye was drawn more into it, and I could see rainbow colors of iridescence in the texture of it. I looked at it, and said, "I think this was a gift."

It totally changed my perspective. That wasn't something that I did. My eye was drawn. Or perhaps something in me was looking for another way, and in its looking found this leaf. Who knows cause and effect? What I know is I was walking, I was dejected, I saw this life, I picked it up. I looked deep into it, and felt healed. And I still have it.

ANDREA: For the future?

CRESS: I may stop teaching aikido altogether to move to a different form. I don't know quite what form, but involving dance more.

I'd stop because, after struggling for two years in my teaching and training to modify the hierarchical/authoritarian model, I want to throw it out and start anew. The model pervades aikido. It shows up in the form and essence of techniques, in the structure of the classes, and in the role of teacher being up here, addressed as "*Sensei*," with the peons down there in a line.

I'm not starting completely anew because I have embodied and learned a tremendous amount from aikido, but I don't want to use the *forms.*

I want to find a way of being holy in myself, and from that place, find a way to cooperate with other people. I don't know how to do that within the forms of aikido, and I'm tired of trying to figure it out.

ANDREA: What sorts of exercises accomplish what you want, yet don't involve aikido?

CRESS: A boundary exercise: have two people stand apart and make contact with one another. One of them agrees to stand where they are, and the other just moves up toward the first. Have the first one say "No," or "Stop," when they are at a comfortable distance.

When I teach this, and people stay in touch with their feelings, what often comes up is fear, anger, and helplessness, and, as they stay with that, and transform it, there is a tremendous sense of self-empowerment that doesn't have anything to do with hurting, pinning, or throwing anyone else.

There's a whole level to work with when somebody does cross my boundary: how I stay with myself. This is a very important thing. We've all had the experience of having our boundaries infringed. We have material to draw on. When somebody tunes into their body and recalls that experience, then they can feel what goes on in their body, and work to find again a place of empowerment. Therapists work to help people resolve grief and family issues, and the family's miles away. They don't need to have the person there.

ANDREA: You said that you still train once a week.

CRESS: And I teach four times a week. My teaching has already moved so far away from classical aikido that I feel uncomfortable using the word "aikido" to describe it. I don't know what I'll call it. Maybe "Exuberance, A Way of Living." Who knows what form this is going to take? I feel passionately that I have something to offer in terms of movement, loving relationship, and self-empowerment, especially for women, but also men.

I want to have a form, and I also know that's a seductive thing. I don't want to impose my form on others. I want to create a space where people can find themselves through movement. Hopefully people will take flames from that candle, and go off and light their own fires elsewhere.

ANDREA: Is there good that you take from your experience of aikido?

CRESS: Yes. I am aware of what violence is. I have a profound experiential understanding of both sides of a conflict, in a gut way that I didn't have before.

I've also gotten from aikido an ability to read energy. I have developed awareness of the initiation of movement before it's reached the physical stage. It is nonphysical. It can move the physical, and it's not physical. I would liken it to light or wind or water.

Aikido gives me the ability to feel more deeply into myself, and into other people from a place of physical contact, and also from a place of perceiving. We all do it. When you're on the phone with a friend, and all of a sudden they become quiet, and you think, "Oh, something's going on." You can't see them or touch them, but you perceive where they are.

I have enhanced that through aikido. I could have enhanced it through body work, dance, gardening, or meditation. Aikido was my route. It's not the only one.

ANDREA: How does body work fit in with what you're doing?

CRESS: Hand in hand. I started aikido first. One of my aikido teachers, at the end of class, would guide us through Kiatsu, which I would describe as a laying on of hands and sensing deeply—to the tissue and bones and structures—what was going on; and moving or allowing energy to flow in a way that would be healing to that part that was injured.

I just knew I wanted to do it more.

A co-worker, who was also doing aikido, was studying acupressure. One day, she held two points on me, and I felt the energy run between them. I said, "Wow. I want to do that." I went to an introductory class, and had the same resonance I had with aikido. I took the program and graduated. Here I am, six years later, with my own bodytherapy practice.

Skills I developed in aikido I brought to my body work: the sense of blending, of allowing the other person to be in the place that they are. When I'm touching the client, I'm not trying to fix them. I'm not trying to make their pain be a bad thing. I'm just hanging out with them. I find, as I do that, magic happens.

ANDREA: What do you mean by "magic"?

CRESS: Healing. Transformation. Change. It's different from the change that happens if I push a bone back in place, smooth a muscle out, or tell it to relax. All of which don't touch the heart of the being I'm working with.

When I can be out of my own way enough so that I can be present in a non-judgmental and loving way, the body moves itself. The tissue moves, and then starts to unwind itself and realign.

ANDREA: What you're describing as "magical" is just being more real.

CRESS: Which is perhaps, after all, what magic is: being very real.

ANDREA: What's most compelling for you about the process?

CRESS: What is deeply moving to me is being present with someone as they get more present with themselves. That's what I love. It's a challenge to me to shut my mouth, or to still my hands long enough to let them just be.

When I let go of my thinking mind's control, and allow my hands to move on a person's body in a way that just feels right, staying attentive, allowing this to happen rather than going in and saying, "This muscle's tight. We should smooth it out," I can think, "This muscle's tight. I wonder what this is about." And dialoguing with the client.

ANDREA: When you say "dialogue," you mean a dialogue with your hands?

CRESS: I mean a nonverbal and a verbal dialogue through whatever channels are available.

If my hands get a "No" from the body, I take my hands away until I don't get the "No." It can be as though I hear it. Or, I might feel the body stiffening, and I change my touch so the body doesn't feel threatened.

ANDREA: You're very articulate and yet you do a body work practice. Why is this? How are they related?

CRESS: I mistrust my own articulateness because I can go off down this wonderful intellectual trail, and leave my feelings, myself, and the other person behind. It's important for me to have words, but have the words come from feeling. I try to allow myself to be in the place of, "I don't know how to put this into words." And let that be, rather than find words and stick them on anyway.

Drawing, movement, music, spirituality, socializing, and intellectual discourse are all channels for communication. The more of these I can use and be open to, the more possibility for growth, creativity and health.

When I'm moving, my mind can go into reporter mode rather than directive mode. So, it isn't saying, "Do this. Do that," or "You did this wrong. You did this badly." It's saying, "I did this. I felt this. This happened."

I get to use that awareness later to help me hone my skills. If I'm in aikido and I'm trying to throw my partner, my mind might say, "Oh, you jerk. You don't know how to do this. You can't learn at all, and you're just trying to muscle through."

Or my mind might say, "I'm going into the flow now. And I'm turning this way. Oh, I'm not in the flow. Now this is happening. Wow. Now this is happening."

Then, my mind is reporting on my experience. That becomes a rich resource for me to remember, and think, "When I didn't push against them, it went easier."

ANDREA: Where do you stand now in relationship to aikido?

CRESS: I feel ashamed that I spent seven-and-a-half years in this martial art, learning to fight and adding fighting energy into the universe. At the same time, I also feel glad to be where I am now. And aikido was part of my journey here. I wish I'd gotten here sooner, but I'm also very appreciative that the path I took taught me more compassion for other people. I don't know how else I could have gotten this compassion, and I love myself for having it.

All I would say is that I'm a being in process. What I say now is pretty much what I've been saying for awhile, and also what I'm saying is changing. My understanding changes. So that, as with everything else in my life, none of this is cast in concrete.

A few months after the interview, when I contacted Cress to take photos for the book, she told me she had made her gi into a laundry bag. She'd fashioned the handles of the bag from the ties of her hakama. A photo shoot occurred near Queen Wilhelmina's Windmill on the western end of Golden Gate Park, right off the Great Highway in San Francisco. It overlooks the Pacific Ocean. As the shutter clicked, the enormous sails of the windmill moved slowly round with the breeze.

Sue Ann McKean

Raised in California and Southeast Asia, SUE ANN MCKEAN *is known for excellence both in aikido and in bodybuilding. Her main aikido teacher was Robert Nadeau. She began studying aikido in 1973. After getting her black belt in aikido, she started weight lifting in 1982 and rapidly rose to become a Miss Olympia contestant—one of the top twenty women bodybuilders in the world. She is a person with enormous physical vitality, eloquence, and depth, qualities which are hard to capture on an audiotape.*

Walking to Sue Ann's apartment door, I saw rugs hanging out to air, a hummingbird feeder, and two ten-pound barbell weights by the door. Her apartment was humble and quiet. There were some books, a futon couch, a VCR. Small magnetized pictures of women bodybuilders hung on the refrigerator door. Some of them were her. The woman who sat across the kitchen table from me in a baggy cream-colored sweater, sweatpants, and thongs didn't look like a person with such muscles. Her toenails were painted light red. She talked about how those pictures have no soul. They were similar to photos you would see on the covers of muscle magazines: the faces of the models have lots of makeup, the models' muscles shine with oil, and somehow looking at those pictures does not touch my heart. And then she showed me some photos that do have soul—portrait studies of Sue Ann by Jan Watson. Jan did the portraits for this book.

ANDREA: Have you always been physically active?

SUE ANN: The physical is my escape. When I was a kid, there was a lot of violence in my family. I lived at the local swimming pool.

Swimming on the team really saved me. I have very vivid memories of times at the swimming pool, the bright and sunny summers in Southern California. My father was in the Marine Corps, so we moved around a lot. I swam in the swim team overseas. I started doing karate when I was in Thailand, and did that passionately.

ANDREA: Were you with your family?

SUE ANN: Just my father. I had to get away from my mother. And I had to get away from Haight-Ashbury, Summer of Love, and 1967. I was feeling, "I'm just a teenager. My life is getting nipped in the bud." So, I asked my father if I could come and live with him. He was in Laos at the time. He said, "OK."

ANDREA: Wasn't there a war there?

SUE ANN: They were fighting thirty miles from where I lived. You could hear the bombs going off. My dad wasn't the most responsible man in the world. I go to Laos, and there are zero kids my age, almost zero Americans. We're not supposed to be there. There are a few guys like him, mercenary pilots, who fly in supplies to the tribesmen who were fighting with the communists. I'm sitting there saying, "Dad, I still have some high school to finish. And where are the kids my age?"

He says, "Oh .... Well, you can take correspondence courses." It was a pit there. I said, "No way." The next suggestion was, "Well, we'll put you in a school down in Bangkok." I went. He took me down, and enrolled me. He was going to stick me in a Baptist youth hostel. Now, I'm a really rebellious kid, I've seen a lot of drugs. I'm a hippie. And I'm not living with a bunch of holier-than-thou rollers. I said, "No." So he put me in a hotel. I lived like a queen: room service, the whole shebang. After a few months, I thought, "This is too expensive." I found an apartment. I was basically on my own, because he lived in Laos. I had to shut off the growing part of me, and become an adult fast. My father was killed—another trauma I put on hold. . . .

ANDREA: What did you do? How did you live?

SUE ANN: For some reason, I wanted to stay after my dad died. I had no guardian. They would have deported me, but my English teacher said, "I'll be your guardian." I said, "Oh, phew, thank you." And so he took over guardianship. My father left tons of travel vouchers, which could be traded in for airline tickets, rental cars, hotels, everything. He had left me months of travelling. I said, "I'm going to take the long way home to California." I figured out a trip through the Middle East and Europe.

When Sue Ann came home in 1970, she moved back in with her mother. "The only way my mother knew to nurture was to feed me a book. She was completely into a spiritual domain." After about ten months there, Sue Ann hitchhiked across the country to Virginia, where she stayed for awhile, and worked in a hotel. The A.R.E.—the Association for Research and Enlightenment was across the street. She said, "I found a bunch of psychics, people who will tell you stuff like, 'You were a cat in another life.'"

SUE ANN: I thought, "This isn't it." It was the early 1970s. I wanted to transcend, evolve, and get out. I was very lost. I roamed around living in five different places in ten months: in hippy communes, in an ashram, with a family that had five kids, and with a bitter divorced woman. I did not know what the hell I was doing. Then I saw a sign on the bulletin board of a health food store that said, "Need a roommate. Call Paul for interview." I moved in. Paul was an aikido brown belt. By this time I thought I was a loathsome hopeless idiot. He was very encouraging to me and said that I had a kind of intelligence I knew nothing about, at least in my head.

ANDREA: What do you mean?

SUE ANN: My body is intelligent and coordinated. I can pick up stuff physically. My body has something. He kept saying, "You have to do aikido." Even though Paul encouraged me, I didn't do aikido for about three months. Finally, I watched a class. I fell in love with it instantly. I thought, "This is what I've been searching for in school. I've been trying to understand this mind/body connection." I had been enrolled in college, studying everything that they offered about

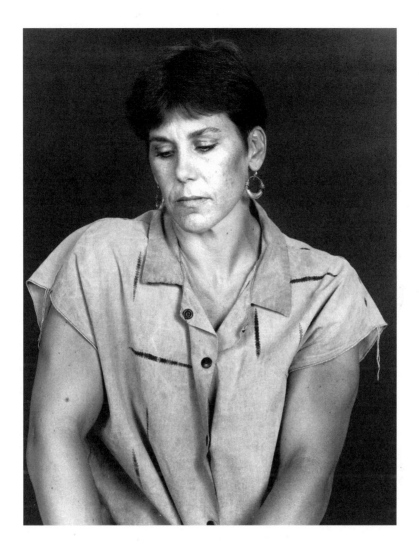

body and mind. I was dis-integrated mentally and physically. I didn't know how to be in my body. I didn't even know I was disembodied. But I knew something was wrong.

In school, they don't teach you about coordination and integration. They say, "Learn these things, and study these books." I became more stuck in my head. Then, I started doing aikido and it was philosophy in action: nonresistance, how to deal with your feelings, and feel a sense of "lineup" or centeredness in relationship to your body, a situation, and another person. In aikido, for the first time in my life, I got a sense of groundedness. I literally felt the ground under me. I had been floating around, searching for a way to fit in, wherever I could get connected. My attention was up and out all over, looking for somewhere to land. In aikido, I feel my feet on the ground. I put my attention down in my feet, and feel that there is real solid support there. The suggestion, if you have a good teacher, is, "Feel your feet. You are here. There is no place else to go. There is Mother Earth supporting you right in this instant." You know, it's an illusion that you're lost and disconnected, an illusion that feels very real. But if you pay attention, right now, you're connected to something real and solid. And in that connection to the earth, you feel connection to the body and beyond. Even though it always mystified me, I received feedback that I had all this bodily presence. I didn't feel I was in my body. I have some psychological training now and I realize that I survived in my family by trying to understand, "Life is crazy and let's try to understand it." But that's a trip down the wrong tunnel. You know, the understanding is in your heart and in your being. Aikido turned me on to something other than concepts and trying to "figure it out." It taught me, "Be. Be present. Be here."

I already knew that life was one big chaotic stress, and people were going to attack me. So how do I deal with the pressure of the world, of a conflict, of someone making a demand on me? My training in my family is to deal with it one way, and my instinct is "fight or flight." If my habitual reaction is to go toward a conflict, then, in aikido, I'm going to get killed by the sword. But as I trained, I learned I had options, "Well, I can move over here, or I can step back." Aikido philosophy says, "Find the place in yourself that knows how to be and deal appropriately with this situation, rather than thinking, 'I always do it this way.'" Aikido taught me how to relax, take it all in, and see everything, "There's the swordsman, but there's also this dimension over here. I can move in that dimension, at my back. I can move straight in." You know when you get that kind of all-seeing feeling? It's so great to have that "Ahh." The blinders go down. Windows open up.

ANDREA: Was this instantaneous or over time?

SUE ANN: Over time. But I saw the potential of aikido in the first few classes. Paul is an impeccable presenter. And my second teacher, Bob, isn't academically trained, but he's articulate, imaginative, and creative. Using his body to demonstrate, he explains things very well. Many teachers just show you a technique. I wouldn't have done it if the philosophy wasn't there.

Paul also introduced me to meditation. I started to do TM and found home in myself. I was starting to feel not-so-crazy. I felt so good on the mat. The person who walked up those stairs to the *dojo* was a totally different person than the one who walked down the stairs. The down side was that I became addicted to the energy. If I came to the *dojo* by myself, I couldn't get it. I needed the teacher, and the class.

ANDREA: Did you want a black belt?

SUE ANN: No, I didn't. I just wanted to feel I was progressing spiritually.

ANDREA: How could you mark that?

SUE ANN: I felt better, more at peace, and connected. "Connection" is a big word for me. I did not feel connected in childhood. All that stuff happened in Thailand. I was just exhausted.

Some people come to train and the first day they say, "When do I get my black belt? How long is it going to take me?" I think, "Never going to make it with that attitude." You can get there if you do the practice day by day as fully as you can. I was not goal-oriented. I'd write some goals down and forget about them. And then I'd end up thinking, "Why am I feeling so unfocused and spaced out?" In aikido, the structure of the school, the teacher, and just the natural process of training every day made me skillful enough to take the test.

ANDREA: Do you remember your test?

SUE ANN: It was in 1977. It was the first time I had to perform. The anxiety just killed me, but I felt good about my test. Bob had trained us well. He always said, "All that is the energy. It means you're getting the energy to do a good job. If you're getting really nervous, it means you're getting a lot of energy." He taught us how to reinterpret. I guess they call it "reframing" now.

ANDREA: Did you want to climb the ranks in aikido?

SUE ANN: I knew if I got a black belt—there weren't very many women black belts then—Bob might make me teach. I thought, "I don't know anything." Because in my head, I didn't know how to do aikido. I would get in my body and then I'd know how to teach fine. I ended up liking teaching and teaching a lot.

In my aikido years, I think that we were working to be more than human, better than human, above, beyond, transcending. It was not about being human. We had this great knowledge and philosophy that the rest of the world didn't have. And we were very superior about our take on "how it all works."

I had developed as much as I could. I was very enmeshed with my teacher, and didn't feel I could do it on my own. I wasn't feeling in touch with myself, my needs, dreams, and desires. I lost myself. I think that is part of the process. You lose yourself, you feel what that feels like. You give yourself over to someone, project your power, your strength, and your creativity on them, and you feel that for awhile.

And then something starts to grow. I was growing in rank, but something inside of me didn't feel like it matched my stature. I projected my qualities onto him: my knowing, my authority, and my taking a stand and saying, "This is the way it is for me." I gave my power away and I was really trying to find it.

ANDREA: How did you reconnect with your own power?

SUE ANN: I started clashing with my teacher. After five years of being a devoted, complying, conforming, great student, I started upstaging him on the mat, trying to level him, and trying to get back at him for "taking my power." Because I had this pattern of giving in and giving up my power for so many years, he was not going to just give it back. In our society, men have the power. They're not going to just give it back. Women have to come from their power. You can't "get it" from men. I saw in that struggle that if I really came from my power, he treated me differently. But instead I was behaving like a little kid, saying, "You don't treat me with respect." What I came to learn was, if I acted like a grown-up, I would be treated like one. But I'm not going to be treated like one when I'm acting like a kid. To grow up, I had to leave. I started bodybuilding in 1982. Through bodybuilding, I started to have a life of my own.

I did aikido for ten years before I got into bodybuilding. At first, just dealing with another person attacking me was so engaging. But after I became a black belt, I was teaching a lot and showing the new people. I was a big fish in a small pond. When I started bodybuilding, it felt like I was a teeny little fish in a big lake.

ANDREA: Do you have a good relationship with your former teacher now?

SUE ANN: We're friends. And we can talk honestly about what happened. I went through a lot of blaming and resentment. He'd get defensive but he hung in there. He doesn't take things too personally. We had long periods of not seeing each other very much. But, he kept in touch. I wouldn't see him for a few months. Then I would find that I felt differently toward him. I started to feel gratitude that I learned a lot from him. Now, I see he's a human being, great and flawed. I can sit and talk with him with no intimidation or guarding myself. I feel like a peer with him. I marvel because it's been fifteen years, and this is what I wanted in the relationship.

ANDREA: What did you see in bodybuilding initially?

SUE ANN: The first show I did, I went out onstage and thought, "They're looking at me! And taking *my* picture. Wow, this is very up-front and real. These bodybuilders aren't afraid of their egos." The tremendous ego rush—Wow, I'm Somebody, I'm important, I'm wanted—was such a hook.

ANDREA: How did you apply aikido to bodybuilding?

SUE ANN: Bodybuilding was a way for me to practice my aikido mental-energy skills in something completely foreign to me. When I'm

backstage, pumping up, getting my muscles ready for the competition, there's a lot of pressure. I'm scared. All the thoughts—"I'm
going to fail," or "I will blow it," or "Don't forget this," and "Do I
look OK?"—are flooding into my mind. Then I do a centering practice that gets me out of my head and into my belly. My energy starts
flowing. I'll spend a lot of time doing two-steps and *ki*-flow practices, instead of the usual pumping-up with weights that the other
bodybuilders are doing. This gets me into a deeper place in myself.
I imagine myself filling up the stage, just like I would on the aikido
mat: "Here comes the three-man attack. OK, I have to own this,
the whole mat, the whole auditorium; and fill it up with my energy.
And blend with these guys attacking me, blend with the audience;
not kill them, and not run away from them, but become one with
them, and love them."

The "reframing" which we talked about earlier served me well
in bodybuilding. I could think, "God, I'm getting nervous. I'm going
to really mess up this time." If, instead, I thought, "I'm going to do
a fantastic job out there because I'm getting so much energy to fill
up this stage. I have to just let it release, let it go, and let it flow
through me," that helped me out a lot. I remember once thinking,
"I am sick of being nervous. I'm so tired of it. I'm not going to be
nervous." I convinced myself so well that I pushed all the energy
down. I went out on stage and did a very flat performance. I thought,
"Bob was right. I pushed the energy and nervousness away and I
gave a dead-ass performance."

I saw a big show as a *randori* —the audience is a thousand-per-
son attack. Aikido trained me to perceive this not as a threat, but
as an opportunity to get bigger, to fill out, to transform, and to go
to another level of myself. That's where my interior skills either
worked for me or they didn't. Competitive bodybuilding performances were an opportunity to play with aikido principles in a non-
aikido form. In bodybuilding competitions, no *uke* was going to
cover my ass. I either got there or I did not. The feedback was ruth-
less if I did not.

When I went to the pro's, the competition was fierce. There are
so many things—insecurities and arrogance—that could pull me out

of myself and into competing, comparing, and judging. Instead of being centered, I was caught up in proving something. I did my Miss Olympia, and I saw it was bullshit, but I didn't know what was next.

I pretended for so long that I loved bodybuilding, that I loved training my ass off five hours a day, and organizing my life totally around my physique. I didn't. I became one of those bodybuilders I promised I would never be: sit down with me, and all I could talk about was my diet, my posing routine, my training, my show, and that I was hungry. I was addicted to exercise, to the applause, and to public opinion. If I got a great review in a magazine, my mood went way up. And if I didn't, I was totally depressed. After a while, I wanted to kill all the fans who just related to my biceps. I ended up saying, "Hey, I am a person. I am a human being. I have feelings. And you treat me like a piece of meat." By not listening to my inner voice saying, "Time to move on," I lost my power in another way in bodybuilding.

ANDREA: What would be the thing you would listen to next time to avoid the downhill slide and just move on?

SUE ANN: I don't see well into the future. Some people have great vision. I jump in and muck around. Then I get out and I say, "Oh, that happened." Then, situations occur that test me. And I think, "Hmm. I learned that." Bodybuilding showed me how malnourished emotionally and spiritually I was, how hungry for attention, and it pointed the way to the next piece of work I had to do. It indicated vast gaps in my development as a human being. And getting in therapy, even more than bodybuilding, helped with that.

ANDREA: What brought you to therapy?

SUE ANN: Three years ago, physically, mentally, and emotionally I went into a big black hole. I couldn't function, my body was shaking, and I was burned out. I couldn't think anymore. I felt dead inside, yet very emotional. I felt like saying: "Someone, save me. Help me. I'm dying." I went to a therapist and told her, "I'm screwed up. I feel like I'm going crazy. I don't know what's next." When I started therapy, it was a shock to me that huge chunks inside—the emotional part of me—had not developed. I thought, "What about all those years of meditation, all those years of hard training?" I decided to become more committed to being an integrated person than a world-class athlete.

I feel lucky I found my therapist. She modeled for me a knowledgeable, strong, wise person who is also human, and doesn't have it all together. I'm grateful I didn't find an I'm-going-to-fix-you therapist. And she's doesn't do the magical, mystical routine of, "Maybe in twenty years, you too can be here like me." Some people let you know the dues they paid and how long it took. They limit you. They brainwash you into thinking you'll be able to feel and be as sensitive as they are if you practice real hard for twenty years.

ANDREA: What are you doing now?

SUE ANN: I'm going to the gym and I'm training people. I also do body work for a living. I'm in therapy. Everything's so mundane. And I know it's part of my work to be comfortable in the mundane too, but I hate it. I want to be in the glorious and the passion, the larger-than-life picture. I guess I'm a drama queen.

ANDREA: Isn't it human to want that?

SUE ANN: A lot of humans are very happy just coming home and watching TV and having a beer. I come home and I watch TV. And I'm finally getting comfortable with it.

I travelled all over the world last year. I feel so myself, so centered, grounded, and expansive, when I'm travelling. It's a clarity that I don't have when I'm home. At home I think, "What am I doing with my life? Where do I go now? What's the point?" In the past I have chosen people, especially men, who provided structure for me. And there's always a lot of interesting weird entangled stuff going on. Not exactly comfortable, not mundane. I'm learning not to latch on to another person to do that work for me. I have to do it myself.

When I ask, "What now?" I know that I still have work to do with gentleness. That's why I'm doing body work. The practice makes me be gentle with myself, and with other people. They're lying there totally vulnerable. At first, it made me nervous dealing with a body just lying there. I thought, "I wish they would attack me. I'd know what to do. What do I do?" Touch 'em. Touch 'em? In aikido, we touched all the time. I loved the touching, but I was covertly getting my touching needs met. I was not really letting another person into my heart. In body work I feel, "My God, this person's vulnerable. I have to get vulnerable. I have to let go of my armor."

It is the next thing in front of me: "Now you need to develop and get more in touch with your sensitivity and your inner feminine side. You know about 'Warrior.' You've played that game out."

ANDREA: What do you mean by warrior?

SUE ANN: When I'm in "warrior," the best part of my warrior, I'm protecting the innocent and the weaker. I can get real protective of women or children. I can kill. And that energy comes right up. I feel like there needs to be a balance in me. I need to become more "gentle": more listening, more feeling, less self-centered, and more supportive. I've got a piece of the warrior archetype, and now I think, "How can I give myself? How can I make a contribution? Where do I fit in? What do I have to give to make this society better?"

I learned in bodybuilding that "feminine" had nothing to do with how you dressed or how you wore your hair; that it is a quality, something within us that's been denied and repressed. I am much more interested in discovering my essential feminine nature within than struggling with men and society to get back what I lost.

ANDREA: For exercise, what do you do now?

SUE ANN: I work out in a gym. I'm teaching aikido again. It's good for me to get back into aikido because I'm getting back into it in a nondependent, nonaddictive way. Maybe now I can contribute something. My questions are not so much, "What do I need?" and "What can I take from the art?" but, "What can I give?"

ANDREA: As a teacher, how do you prevent students from forming a destructive attachment?

SUE ANN: I played a lot with that last year. The students really wanted an authority figure. They'd come to my classes and I'd be very let-it-all-hang-out human. I felt they didn't like that. A couple of women did the starry-eyed syndrome with me, looking at me like, "Wow, you're so great." There's too much of a recognition of myself and my past. I thought, "Too bad, gang. I'm not going to let you project your fantasies. If you want a teacher who is descended from the gods, go to someone else's class." I felt a little defensive about it. If I sensed a student had the need for an ultimate authority, I'd start denigrating myself. I would trip myself up to let them know how imperfect I am. I don't do that now. It's not powerful. I'm just myself.

Kathy Park

KATHY PARK *was born in Washington, D.C., in 1951 and raised on the East Coast. Her main aikido teachers have been Frank Doran, Robert Nadeau, Richard Heckler, Wendy Palmer, Hiroshi Ikeda, and Terry Dobson, among others. She teaches aikido and sculpts in Healdsburg, California. At the time of the interview, she was about to begin volunteer work at a women's prison. She currently is co-director of the Prison Integrated Health Program, an innovative volunteer program of holistic health practices serving the women incarcerated at FCI Dublin, the federal prison. She administers the program as well as doing individual sessions of body work on the women. At the prison, she also runs a long-term stress management group and teaches somatic education to a small group of healers and body workers.*

When I interviewed Kathy, she and her husband, Henry, were living in a basement apartment in her mother's house in Berkeley. They were in the process of finding a new place to live, in the country.

As I walked downstairs into the main room, I noticed incense, but as time wore on I didn't notice it at all. It was cool and dark, in contrast to the sunny day outside. We sat in her bedroom, I on the floor, she on the bed. There were many small lovely voluptuous sculptures of women around her apartment—in the sun on the windowsill, and a few under the bed.

She wore a lavender patchwork jacket and trousers. The tape recorder perched wobbling on a three-legged chair. Recovering from a pulled muscle, at times she sat up straight and full-postured, and at times she reclined. Her face is very mobile; in each angle there is a different beauty. Her expressive hands form shapes I understand. About halfway through the interview, we stopped for a cup of tea, and Kathy loaned me a white handmade blanket because I had gotten cold.

During our talk, I frequently looked to the window, where hanging from the ceiling by a thread was a large wicker sculpture of a woman on a winged horse.

Kathy started doing aikido in Oregon in 1977. She was living on a little farm with her boyfriend and several other people.

ANDREA: Why did you start doing martial arts?

KATHY: My boyfriend, David, got involved with karate. David's teacher was a cop who had *shodans* in karate, aikido, and judo. He'd been in Korea in the military police, and had all these weird weapons, guns, and hunting arrows. Strange guy.

David would practice around me, and practice with me.

ANDREA: With your consent?

KATHY: No. In a way that was infuriating to me because he would flick punches a quarter inch off of my head. Or kick, and then pull the kick at the last moment. I felt invaded and powerless. I didn't like feeling what I was feeling. I bit into the idea that martial arts would give me the skill, the finesse, the self-confidence, and the control to get it more together so I wouldn't feel the pain of our relationship deteriorating.

We both got real involved with this teacher, and with a whole cult of people that were around him. It's not a relationship I would invite into my life now. I don't want to give over that measure of control. But I did then. There's a tradition in the martial arts, that is definitely part of my lineage, to give it over to a teacher. It's no mistake that it was a male teacher—very charismatic, handsome, powerful, mysterious, juicy, a little kind of subterranean sexual-something-or-other floating around. It never came out in any real sense, but it was there.

ANDREA: What did you want from him?

KATHY: I wanted power, confidence, and chops—so that I could get David back. Also, it felt good to be not only recognized, but challenged. There was enough innate skill, or willingness inside me, that I could feel my teacher actively engaged in cultivating that. I wanted to respond, to do well, to have him think well of me. Plus there was something, in the purest sense, in the karate philosophy that appealed to me: making a connection with the universe and using that to defuse a situation; also realizing that there was virtue in not fighting.

Mostly we did karate, and a little bit of judo. I had no other context for the aikido that he was doing. It looked sort of like pretzel dough. It was all wound up in this strange stuff.

I remember one particular instance where David and I were going to fight in a match. We're in a relationship that's not doing real well. This is karate therapy? I wouldn't recommend it to anybody. There were three phases to it. In one phase, David was very aggressive, all over me scoring points. It was coming too fast. I couldn't block anything. I couldn't see it coming. It completely knocked me off. Then there was a pause, and a regrouping. In the second phase, he didn't attack, but he made himself impenetrable. I attempted to attack and couldn't get in anywhere. I was rattling inside. Not only could I not defend myself but I couldn't get in, I couldn't touch. And in the third phase, I forget exactly what he did. By then I was undone. I was crying. And I had an incredible visceral vision that my center was outside of my body, spilled on the floor in front of me; I was completely disconnected from my center.

It was a wake-up for me. I thought, "This is not good for you, Kathy. Stop doing this. This is not the direction to go."

Partly out of that experience, Kathy took a yearlong break from Oregon. In late 1977, she moved down to Berkeley, lived with her sister, and started studying at Aikido of Berkeley.

KATHY: Aikido was something that fit my mind, my emotions, and my body. I went to all the easy classes and stayed for all the hard classes. I came back bruised, and loving it. I rewarded myself with cookies and hot baths. I felt like I had found a community. Whatever had been decimated up in Oregon was being built up again. None of the teachers here had that cult charisma. It was straightforward: just come to the class, and you're going to work with everybody. Some people you'll like working with, and some you won't. That's part of the practice. There are beginners and senior students. Just put yourself in it and do it.

By that time I was a blue belt. I was feeling so good that I started to filter that back into my relationship with David. We agreed to give it another try. I went up to Oregon for another year. It started off fine. As a brand-new blue belt, I was able to teach and explain basic aikido ground-level exercises better than my teacher in Oregon. To his credit, he recognized that. So I began teaching.

Because I have enough inherent grandiosity, I used to think that, as a teacher, I would be able to see something that someone else couldn't see. I thought of a teacher as sort of omniscient and omnipotent. In that realm, I'd never talk about it of course, because I humble-pied myself all over the place; but now I don't want that kind of adoration or power.

ANDREA: When you teach, how do you stay humble, genuinely, not just putting on the face of it?

KATHY: That dovetails into the question: how do you empower other people to take care of themselves? It's very basic. Whose power, whose responsibility, whose job is it to push somebody into new territory, or to learn something, and face something difficult? It can get weird and warped if I think that it's my job to make you face something about yourself. Maybe that's the realm of a therapist with her client. So, when I teach, I emphasize: "Look there's this phenomenon which is called, 'Overriding your basic information.' Some of that information is about limitations."

It's your job, as a student, to learn how to do a high fall when you want to. You come to me and say, "OK, I'm ready." It's not my job to decide you're ready, and then spring it on you.

In my training in Oregon, however, this is the type of "compliment" my teacher would pay me: I was teaching a technique. David was my *uke*. I mentioned that this technique, throw, and the wrist turn, would work fine if the attacker had a knife. Out of the corner of my eye, I see my teacher walk over to his big black bag. He comes back with a sharp eight-inch stiletto. He hands it to David, and says, "Attack."

Here's my soon-to-be-ex-lover. I think, "God damn, one more of these situations where he's pointing something at me." We're in this totally threatening weird situation. I took care of it. I disarmed him and took it away. I totally had the shakes afterwards. Our teacher did camps with us, too. We'd catch arrows. Shoot .357 magnums into watermelons, so that we could get a real sense of what would happen to a person's head. It was sort of an interesting education.

ANDREA: For what purpose?

KATHY: To develop a real respect—including fear—of the power of these weapons. Our teacher had respect for realism, even though he was an incredible romantic. There was something very good about what he exposed us to. I'm glad I have training in another martial art. Throughout the years that's helped me to survive on the mat, and to correct horrible punches from aikido people, who've never learned how to punch. I learned something about lining my whole self up behind my right knuckle. Being able to break a board, to deliver that much energy to one spot in order to accomplish a certain task, feels useful to me.

In 1978, Kathy came back to Berkeley. Partly she left because her relationship was over. Aikido and the body work that she'd gotten into were both lifesavers. She grabbed them. It didn't seem possible to pursue those things and be in Oregon.

KATHY: And also there was a quality of, "This town's not big enough for the two of us." I don't regret it at all. I immersed myself again in Aikido of Berkeley, and then in Turk Street Dojo in San Francisco. I got my black belt in 1980. I was about to turn thirty. I thought, "I should do it now. My body is the strongest it's going to be. I have the time, the teachers, and the willingness. It's going to take a big chunk of energy, time, commitment. Do it now."

A week before my test I saw a baby's birth. That was very helpful. Everything changed perspective. I coasted through the last week of training. I thought, "If I don't have it inside my body, one more week isn't going to do it. Besides, I just saw a baby be born. Now I have an idea of what's really important."

ANDREA: The test was almost anticlimactic?

KATHY: In a way it was. I think tests should be anticlimactic, they're simply an affirmation of what is already true.

I did a practice before the test where I imagined having a black belt. I put it on. I thought of myself as a black belt. Partly that came to me as something to do, and my peers and elders said, "That's a good idea. That's a good practice." I took the test from the place of, "I am already a black belt." It wasn't a great test. I remember sitting there in the line of candidates and Frank Doran, one of my teachers, came over and commented on my shade of green. He was teasing. He was trying to make me feel better but it was hopeless at that point. It was a relief to get it over with. I felt that by the time I got to the multiple attack—the first rendition of it wasn't great— I had just woken up and gotten there. I was surprised they cut me off. I felt, "Oh, it's over. Oh, OK, I guess I passed."

One of my friends came up from LA and gave me a birthday black belt party. She said that I was committing to myself. In hindsight I can see that was true. A lot of things happened after the black belt that led me deeper to myself, and, as a result, I eventually found my mate. In some way, before I married someone else, I had to marry myself.

ANDREA: In your training, how did you stay detached from your teachers?

KATHY: To whatever extent I was able to do that, it was because I stayed back. I knew getting close to my teachers would be too scary for me. I learned that there's power to be derived from honoring my fear, simply because it's true. I wasn't entirely or consistently successful, but I tried to strip away the self-judging voices in me which said, "There's nothing to be afraid of." It became clear to me: I'm not going to be one of the people who hang out after class. I'm not going to get involved with wanting personal strokes from some of these teachers.

ANDREA: Did you learn that from training with your teacher in Oregon?

KATHY: I was still recovering from this difficult relationship with David. I decided it was not safe for me to get involved with any man on a needy level. I learned to say to myself, "It's OK if you fucked up, if you're crying, if you're not together, or if you're confused." My needs were met by my involvement with the body work school and the training. In the aikido training, I felt, "I can find solace by knowing if I practice, devote myself to it, and keep coming back, some sense will start to permeate."

Aikido for me was, if not a sitting meditation, a moving medita- tion—a deepening, seeing what in my life could build my ground, and going toward those. For instance, art was always a big part of my life, but I don't think I really understood that it is who I am and where I come from. The aikido metaphor helped me see that.

In 1981, Kathy felt up to her eyeballs with the Bay Area. She wanted to go deeper into her art, and that involved going to the desert. At that point, she was still single, celibate, and lonely. She moved to the desert because she had an uncle-in-law who lived in the Mojave desert, and was a stone sculptor. She knew she wanted to carve. At that point, she packed up all her stuff and put it in a friend's garage.

KATHY: I knew I wanted to get away. There was something about going to the loneliest place I could think of, in order to face the loneliest place inside of me, something about *irimi,* entering into my fear. I grabbed it as a metaphor.

I went off on this quest, and worked with the idea that if I ran into doubt, on any level, I'd turn that into artwork. I produced a lot of work. I also worked on saying, "No." I think that's important, not only in a general health context, but, specifically for people who do aikido to be clear about. Aikido attracts a person who gets off on some aspect of the philosophy of: nobody loses, it all comes out nicey-nicey. "No" seemed to stop the flow and be aggressive.

ANDREA: Aggressive has a pejorative connotation?

KATHY: Absolutely. We get the idea that "blending" and "going with it" all mean "Yes." There's power and truth to be derived from "No." While I was in the desert, people would want things from me. They'd want someone to listen to them, help them with a project, or just someone to share a beer with. I perceived it as having nothing to do with why I was there, and having everything to do with them asking me to join them in their misery. I practiced saying, "I'm not available. I'm not interested in helping you. No."

This felt scary. Some inner battle came up about it: "You arrogant white privileged bitch. How dare you? Don't you know your job is to help everybody?" I had an internal discussion about what my job was, and whether it was even on my job description to take care of me. I put it on my job description. That was the beginning of taking care of me. If that bent somebody else out of shape, that was their problem.

However, I also started to delude myself with the idea that I wasn't going to need a lover or friends. My picture of "Kathy the Warrior" was that being a warrior involved not needing. I was meditating, taking walks, and having a good drink every night. I was in altered states often, if not through chemical stuff, then through this awesome desert. One way information comes to me is I hear words. I'm sitting in meditation, and the voices said: "Kathy, you are not a hermit. Your work, your pleasure, is around people. It's time to find your mate." I'd think about the city that the voices told me to go to, and I'd think about the aikido teacher there, and I'd get adrenalin rushes in the pit of my stomach. At the time I thought that to feel that level of excitement and fear meant, "Oh, I should go toward that." I was taking the entering, *irimi* notion a little too far. Any time I felt intense fear or excitement that meant I was supposed to go toward it? But I felt devoted to the information that was coming through.

In hindsight, I see that these intuitive voices were guiding me away from hermitage and this ridiculous dead-end notion that I was beyond needing a lover or friends, and toward the hard work of relationship, specifically finding my mate. If the excitement or fear of training with that teacher got me there, those intuitive voices weren't complaining.

Following her intuition, in 1982, Kathy moved to the city where her intuition guided her. She started training with an aikido teacher

*there, who told her that he was going to make a real black belt out
of her. The teacher was a young, powerful man from a traditional
school.*

KATHY: The sense that I got of his invitation was that in order to
"make a black belt" out of me, to get all this "California garbage"
out of the way, he was going to put me through the wringer.

If you got him as a partner on the first go-round, he was your
partner for the entire hour. I had been avoiding him. One time, I
was his *uke* for the first technique which involved simply meeting
a strike with your own upward-rising forearm. As soon as the technique was given to the class, I heard his voice saying, loudly and
clearly, "Kathy-san." I gulped. I knew I had him for the rest of the
hour. In the first ten minutes I was bruised completely up and down
my forearm—great big eggs—because his strike was so strong. I
had to endure this (some way I was blowing it?) because no way
were we going to stop and discuss it. That seemed unavailable to
me. My mind started to go into panic and heavy-duty questioning.
What came up for me was, "This is crazy. This is sick. I don't want
to do this. This is painful. I don't want to go through this." I survived the hour, but I did not triumph into another realm. I was crying and on the verge of throwing up at one point. It was awful.

Background to this: by this time I had met Henry, my husband-
to-be. After a long time of not having a lover, I had a lover. I was
being touched gently, sweetly, and softly. These two experiences, this
very difficult ordeal with the teacher, juxtaposed against what was
starting to open up in my life, made it very clear to me which to go
toward. It felt like choosing lovers. I felt like aikido, as it was available to me there, was a hard, demanding, cruel lover. When I compared that to what Henry was offering me, the choice was obvious.

I took a two-year hiatus from aikido. I went through inner dialogue, "Oh, you're chickening out. You're terrible. You are a horrible California aikido person. You aren't a martial artist." That felt
like mental chatter. I had followed my heart. My heart and my body
were quite clear on what was happening.

What came out of Kathy's break from aikido was backyard classes. She started to teach "Aikido as a Metaphor" to a small group of people who were interested in the "goodies" of aikido, and not interested in becoming martial artists. That seemed to her to be worth teaching. At that point, her own brand of teaching started.

Then, Kathy and Henry decided to move to the Mojave desert. Both of them plunged into their art. (Henry's a painter.) They lived in a town of forty people for two years, and did their art full-time. Kathy returned to California several times to train. People gave her consistent feedback that her energy was more deeply embodied.

KATHY: I was much more settled. I was much more powerful. That was an incredible affirmation: "It's about going toward who I am, not about striving and not about something out there, ahead of me, unreachable. It is about going deep inside of myself. That will translate whether or not I dress in my *gi* and *hakama* and train." I said, "All I've been doing is carving stone."

They'd say, "Jeez. It feels like you've been training like crazy."

We ran out of savings so we both got jobs at a local community college. My job was teaching aikido, which was a totally new experiment for this fairly conservative town. I had to show them a University of California at Santa Cruz catalog that has aikido in it in order to prove this was not weird. They were worried. I taught for two years. "Introduction to Aikido," "Intermediate Aikido." I was mostly working with young men, half of whom wanted to fulfill their gym credit to get through college, and half of whom wanted to increase their self-confidence and ability to control themselves. The college catalog listed my married name, K. Woolbert. I knew by the looks on faces coming in the first night that half the men who came expected Kevin Woolbert, or Keith, or Killer. I'd lose a lot of them on that. Then, I taught metaphorical aikido: "Conflict Resolution Through Aikido," which was more talking, reading, and easy physical exercises.

Since it was my class, I gave myself latitude. I'd say, "I'm not much on control. I don't think going for control bears fruit. I think going for dynamic balance does." I had them write essays.

ANDREA: For a phys. ed. class?

KATHY: My intention was to inspire them to use aikido in their lives. The essays were a way for me to get feedback on how or if that was happening. Some of the essays I got back were wonderful. I assigned one about what center is. One guy wrote, "I used to be a really aggressive driver, and I'd cut people off, and I'd flip them the bird. And I'd get angry if someone was driving like an asshole. Now after this class and feeling my center more, it doesn't bother me when people cut in front of me and do stupid things. I don't flip them the bird any more, I don't even get angry."

I felt, "I'm getting across. Aikido is getting across."

The town's reason for existence is the China Lake Naval Weapons Center. To introduce aikido into that community felt risky. But also very sweet.

Going through difficulties in that teaching, I started to feel, "I'm a *nidan*," which I have not formally tested for, and, at this point, probably won't. But I started to feel inside that I was.

The shift occurred as the result of my interactions with a man in my class who got injured, and had a paranoid reaction to it. The agent of the injury was, I think, in the right. He was doing what I set up the class to do. Injuries happen. We'd signed waivers of liability. I had impressed upon everyone that they have to be responsible. I gave a huge rap at the beginning of the semester. I hate it when injuries happen because it plugs me into my ongoing desire to be godlike and prevent it. But that's impossible. Anyway, this guy had such a bad reaction that he ended up making threatening phone calls to the other student and to me.

For me there was something about recognizing abuse, which I have not recognized a lot in my life. When he was threatening me over the phone, I understood as it was happening and told him I would not tolerate this, that it was not OK with me. I told whoever I needed to tell at the school, and the situation was dealt with appropriately. It feels to me like recognizing abuse for what it is and handling that difficult situation with as much breadth and depth as it required, have something to do with the quality of *nidan*.

Then, Henry wanted to go back to school, so we came back out to California. We're still finishing that. Even though there are a million aikido teachers here, I figured there was a niche for me. My classes are quite slow. We discuss things. I ask for questions, for problems. It feels right to me to encourage being present with what you're learning. That's partly in reaction to how I learned, the gung-ho approach.

Kathy returned to the Bay Area in 1989. She trained quite a bit. She was getting invitations, direct and indirect, from her teachers, to go on for her nidan *test.*

KATHY: I realized, "Actually, as far as *nidan* goes I don't care." It's been interesting to stand in that stance of: "No, I'm not interested in testing," in the face of the pressure of people saying, "Look, Kathy, you should."

It's not interesting to me to test. This comes in part out of my questioning and not participating in some of the traditions. For example, in my class, we don't bow in the formalized line like other *dojos* do. We bow in as a semicircle. I'm part of the line. I want it to become more and more circular. The circle denotes much more equality than the straight line, with one person out in front. I'm not comfortable with that hierarchy, with what it evokes, be it power-tripping on my end or giving over power on the student's end.

I don't know if I want to keep bringing along "Kathy the Aikido Teacher" as an equal interest to my art and my body work. If it were a strict career decision, logic would tell me, "It would be good to go for your *nidan,* because that's adding to your résumé." But that feels false. I'd go for my *nidan* because I wanted it. How do I know when I want it? There's a deep, "Yes, I want this." The whole body, the whole system turns toward it and says, "I want this."

Now, I keep putting my aikido involvement in the diminutive. I teach a "little" bit. I'm "sort of" involved. I characterize my aikido involvement as small, not as central as it was.

In addition to realizing that I don't care about getting my *nidan,* I realized that I want to be an artist. I want to devote myself to that, make my living through that, spend most of my time doing that.

Just because I'm good at other things doesn't mean that I should do them. This has been a homecoming for me: "Never mind whether I'm good at it. That's not deep enough. Do I want it?" I think, "Am I going to stop teaching aikido this summer when I go away? In the fall we're hoping to move somewhere else in the Bay Area. Why keep the class going?"

ANDREA: How does the aikido process tie into art?

KATHY: I am an artist. People look at a sculpture and they say, "God, how did you do that?" To me, it's one chip at a time. I start and keep going and then I'm done. There's something about aikido too. "How can you do that?"

"Well, I started, and I went, and I practiced. I chipped away at this. One day, here I am. I am a black belt." There's nothing mysterious about it. Practice. It's very mundane. I use that word not to devalue it, but to make it more accessible.

ANDREA: How do you get paid for doing what you love?

KATHY: How do you make your passion be what supports you in life? What, physically, and in every other way, supports you? The hypothesis that I'm living on, is that it has to do with lining up: if I line up to what I'm about, there's an inherent wedge shape and that means movement is possible. Does the universe respond? I don't know. I'd like to think that the universe responds favorably. So far so good. It goes back to that adage of "Be careful what you ask for because you'll get it." That's a statement about alignment, too. To state that I want this means that I'm lining up to it. I'm directing myself to it. Something magnetic happens when I say that. Some movement happens. Some attraction.

I followed the voice I heard which told me to move, knowing one of the reasons was to find my mate. I was making myself available to being found. I was lined up to that task.

ANDREA: What do you want for yourself?

KATHY: I've been working in these tiny, tiny little places, and I'd love a much bigger studio, and money enough so that I can immerse myself in the way that I'd like to in my art. I'd like more clarity on a number of things. I'd like a nice place to live that I can afford that has a garden space and is quieter and sort of on the fringes of the Bay Area. I'd like Henry to have a good teaching job nearby. I'd like to keep developing community. I'd like to feel free to either continue being involved in aikido or not, and not beat myself up around whatever I decide. Those are a few things. I'm not even mentioning what I'd like for the world. That seems real long-term to me. I don't think we're ready for peace. I don't know what it's going to take, but it seems to hinge on so much inner work. God, do we have time to do that?

As I left, I touched the smooth dark back of a small sculpture of a cougar-like man. I said to her that it seemed like a prototype of something to be carved on a huge scale. She confirmed that she worked this sculpture on a small scale because her studio space is tiny. When I next spoke with Kathy, she and Henry were in the process of moving to a house they found on the Russian River, up north. In her voice, I could hear the relief that she will have a studio, light and spacious.

Diana Daffner

DIANA DAFFNER *was born in Stevenstown, New York, in 1946 and grew up on a farm. She graduated from Cornell University with a B.A. in English Literature and Psychology in 1968. She has worked as a massage therapist and instructor, a workshop leader and instructor in energy massage and awareness, as well as a micro computer trainer. She currently is a project manager and technical writer in the human resources industry, and a t'ai chi chih instructor. She lives on an island off the coast of western Florida with her husband Richard. Her main aikido teacher was Robert Nadeau.*

When I contacted Diana Daffner by phone to set up the interview, she had just come inside after a moonlit canoe ride among the mangrove trees. I expressed my admiration for her athleticism, and she was quick to pierce my illusions: "I wasn't paddling. I was perfectly content to be a passenger." She added, "I am Queen Wimp. I have skinny little toothpick arms. If I could get a black belt, anyone can." As a not-very-athletic person myself, I found this encouraging.

A few weeks later, I sat in my little studio apartment in California and spoke with her long distance in western Florida. She talked a little about her surroundings before we began: "I'm sitting on a glider—an old-fashioned porch couch—and I'm looking through my screen at a canal, and the birds are chirping away. Actually, I don't really see much except greenery. When a boat goes by, I'll see a little bit of the mast. The weather's gorgeous. It's breezy. The bugs here put New York cockroaches to shame."

Diana was introduced to aikido through a week-long workshop Bob Nadeau gave at the Esalen Institute in 1971. At that time she *was on the massage staff there. The workshop was about energy awareness and meditation, not aikido.*

At that time, she was living in Big Sur in a 1946 Dodge pickup truck with a redwood camper, stained glass windows, and a big furry dog. The staples of her life were what she calls "the three M's: massage, music, and meditation." After the workshop, she moved up to Mountain View, and studied with Bob full-time from December 1971 to April 1982. She said, "I didn't do aikido as a hobby."

In 1982, she went back East to be with her father as he was dying. While there, she met Richard Daffner, and in 1983, after her father's death, she moved to New York City to be with Richard. They married in 1985. She worked in the corporate world of New York for many years. Recently, she and Richard moved to Florida, where she teaches t'ai chi chih and other related workshops. She also occasionally trains with the local aikido club.

ANDREA: What was so compelling about that first workshop that you would just pick up and move?

DIANA: When I did the workshop, I discovered that he knew more than I did about energy. He seemed, through his body and his being, to not only be able to describe my energy space, but also to assist me in recognizing it as well. I had profound meditation experiences during that week that were conscious and present, and I wanted more of that.

I was not attracted to Bob for his personality. Nor was I falling in love with him. I was drawn to the work he was doing, and to his ability to teach what he seems to know and experience about energy.

My only previous martial arts experience was that I'd signed up for a judo class in college. I went for a few lessons, and then I had a car accident and injured my back. When I came back to class, they were rolling over a body in the middle of the mat. This is still something I don't like doing. I hadn't learned to roll yet. I wouldn't even attempt it. So, I was kicked out of the judo class. I don't know why I tried judo in the first place.

I started doing aikido because that was part of how Nadeau taught about energy. I got a *gi*, and started going to classes. Once again, I was confronted with having to roll forward on a mat.

I am not a jock. I am not and never have been an athletic person. Rolling forward was a big thing for me. The old Mountain View *dojo* had *tatami* mats. These mats were hard. We had a couple of soft padded mats we called "granny mats" that we would drag out for new people. I rolled on a granny mat for a year.

My *nage* (or partner) would get me into position, and I would say, "Let me take my own fall." I wouldn't let anyone throw me. I was terrified of being out of control, having someone push me before I was ready to go. That's where I started in aikido.

From 1971 to 1982, aikido, meditation, and her work in massage were Diana's world. Anything else she did, like having fun socially, played second fiddle. Aikido training took place every day.

DIANA: Bob's aikido for me was about using aikido to practice being in other spaces of awareness, to practice being. What interested me most about aikido was how it was able to reflect, on a physical dimension, my inner state of mind, my awareness. The aikido gave me immediate feedback on my alignment with flow. That was Bob's gift, showing us how to use aikido in this way.

Most of the years of training were about the deep source of power that is available to us; that we have access to a very deep spiritual sense of ourselves. If you saw me as I was saying this, you'd kind of see me going under, going down to a place of incredible power, a place that seems to scare a lot of people, but a place that's roomy and attractive.

ANDREA: Coming up from that, what did you bring with you? What changed about your sense of yourself?

DIANA: I always had a very light, loving self. When I was a teenager, I experienced the love as a truth. I experienced a powerful love that I had no idea what to do with. I knew that it was not meant for just another person. It was too big for that. I knew that someday I would get back to that love.

During the years that I was doing aikido, my light and loving self was not the major component. But it didn't disappear. It was still

there. Now, I'm more open and accepting of people who haven't gone into their own depth, but who are light and loving. I'm more accepting of people than I was during my aikido training. I had a definite prejudice toward deep and dark, that kind of power; and against light, and what I would have called "airy-fairy."

What I mean by the deep and dark power is that a real tangible power manifests as human beings. There's a power that each of us can access. That power can manifest gently. It doesn't necessarily manifest gruffly. I don't know what the right word would be. It may not be an outward power, it may manifest as an inward power. The power to receive is a power. To put out is a power. These are all different kinds of power, not gender-based, but yin-yang.

ANDREA: Can you talk more about that power?

DIANA: My sense during the days of aikido training was that power has its own intelligence. And given a vessel, a way to manifest, that power will handle all situations. I had a sense that this energy would simply come through, and allow everything to live more in harmony. A lot of time and training was spent learning to trust that power that would then come up and through our bodies and our hands and perform the action.

It always amazed me how when I got really deep, when I let my energy go down to touch that, I also kind of came up—this sounds scary—as my partner as well, as something bigger than both of us, coming up and experiencing my partner's energy from a place underneath them.

To play with that power, that energy, was extraordinary to me. I was first introduced to the truth of it, to the power of my simply being relaxed, through Harvey, Catherine Tornbom's husband.

We were doing a technique in which the wrist is bent, and it's held in such a way that the person really can only go down on their knees. Otherwise, they're going to be in severe pain.

I had his wrist locked into this position, and he was being strong. We tended to be very strong with each other to force our partners to connect with a space that would come from deeper, and to be able to handle it. We chose that rather than being loose and easy all the time.

So there was Harvey with his wrist locked, and there I was. Our instructions, in the training, were to "Hold firm with the hands, but to let everything else be very relaxed. Be relaxed through the knees and the feet. Be very comfortable in the rest of your body, and not be concerned about your partner. Simply drop down into your own space."

Suddenly, as I'm doing that, Harvey is bending down in front of me. I am not "doing" the technique, not forcing him down. I'm only in my own relaxation and my own place. I got so awed by the power of it that I started jumping up and down, going, "Oh, this is so great," still keeping his wrists twisted at the same time. I forgot he was there. It was not as much fun for him. He was immobilized by my grip, and looked like he wanted to kill me. It's one of those moments that you remember.

Aikido is great for giving the tangible feedback, showing us that being relaxed and centered really is powerful. And then there's the sense of coming up behind someone or next to someone to do a technique; and that simply by my opening up in all the pores of my body, my partner falls down. This was always astounding to me.

ANDREA: Ranking and belts weren't important for you?

DIANA: No. I've never been competitive, and never needed marks. In aikido, I never had any rank. Bob didn't test in the early days.

After I had been training a long time, but before I got my black belt, I was determined to learn how to *sutemi*. I believe the Japanese meaning of *sutemi* is to give up your life or some kind of sacrifice. It is the forward fall that's done without touching the mat. The difficult part occurs when your entire body is off the ground, your feet are in the air, and someone else is holding onto your wrists. It's not a big deal for most people. That is, for most people who choose to do aikido. For me, my first *sutemi* was a real learning experience. We were in the Mountain View *dojo* on a granny mat. My partner was kneeling on the mat, and I had a hold on his wrists. Suddenly I was in the air, and this feeling of incredible exultation came over me: "Wow! This is great." At the height of that experience (this happened quickly because I wasn't in the air very long), I heard another voice in my head say, "Oh, no, you don't like *sutemis*." And I thought, "Who is that?" So, doing a *sutemi* taught me that there can be a yes and a no in me at the same time. It's my choice which voice I listen to.

ANDREA: Does anything stand out about your training for your black belt test?

DIANA: When I was training for my black belt, after class one day Bob called upon me to attack him. I don't know how long it lasted. When Bob was really on, he was so powerful that the power frightened me. I was afraid that I'd pull back from the power and get hurt. But I continued to get up from each fall and come back in and attack him. The tears were pouring down my face the entire time. I had never been so stretched to keep going with the energy—beyond my fear—as I was that afternoon.

I was determined to do it. I knew that I was crying. Like when I did that first *sutemi,* there were voices in me screaming that I didn't want to do it, that I had absolutely no interest in doing it. They were probably trying to stop me, but I was so determined that I kept doing it. I knew that other people were watching. I was only vaguely aware of them.

I realized afterward that it looked like he had, someone said, "wiped up the mat with me." It looked like he had been very mean, but he wasn't. He had shown me that I could keep coming in, that I could commit and stay with it, and that I didn't get hurt.

I hit the mat hard, and I might have been sore, but I was not hurt.

When I went up for my black belt test, I would not have been surprised if I had been asked to *uke,* be the attacker instead of just the defender demonstrating aikido techniques. It was not ever done, but among the teachers, I had a reputation as a wimp in terms of *ukemi,* the art of falling.

The *uke* I chose for my black belt test, Jack Wada, had power that is very warm, calm, and embracing. It never threatened me. I was happy he was my *uke* because if I were asked to demonstrate some *ukemi,* he would have been the *nage.* I would be comfortable coming in on him.

As it turned out, my test, as *nage,* was very good. No one asked me to do the falls. Afterward, it was mentioned that having me test as *uke* had been considered. But it would have been all right that day. It would have been fine.

ANDREA: What did your black belt test mean to you?

DIANA: Bob has a calligraphy scroll by O'Sensei, the founder of aikido, that says, "Do the aikido that cannot be seen with the human eye." That was the motto for my years of training. My goal, if there were a goal, was to experience aikido from the place that O'Sensei was coming from, not how he described it afterward, as technique and form.

When I asked Bob if I could go up for a black belt test, he told me, "Yes," but that I had to realize that now, from that moment, till the day of my test, I had to focus on doing the aikido that could be seen with the human eye, which meant perfecting form. In San Francisco, the black belt candidates are examined by a board of high-ranking teachers who all have different philosophies. They are not looking to see if you are manifesting spirit, loving your *uke,* or tapping into universal power. They're looking to see if you are doing good aikido. I had to develop the ability to practice the techniques as they are standardly done, and do that consistently.

Why was it important for me to have the black belt? I'm not sure, but I'm really glad I did it. I needed the recognition of passing the test. It's not often that I have gone after trophies. I wanted to have a black belt.

The black belt also has been useful as a degree, a credential. People are impressed with this concept of black belt.

ANDREA: Did it change training afterward?

DIANA: I went back to using aikido as a tool for awareness, and I had no interest in getting higher ranks. It was enough to take that test to prove after all those years to myself and to everyone, that I could do it just like anyone else. I really liked my test. I felt good afterward. And I was glad that I passed. I'm not sure what other meaning it had. I didn't go out to become a teacher.

In aikido the years just went by. My memory of training is about two things. It's about the people that I trained with. We were dedicated to the process of being. We had similar interests and awareness. And we were able to bring that to training and share with each other. To be willing mirrors for each other. To be trainers for each other in ways that were astounding, fun, and wonderful, and

I loved it.

The other thing that kept me interested in aikido was that moment of connection, that moment of connecting with my own source, of letting go to a larger force, which was going to make things happen. We used to talk about getting out of the way and letting "it" do the technique.

But we were never totally out of the way. Connecting with "it" does the technique. Through that place, I learned how deep a connection I can have with another human being, and how when I connect there, it just feels like we're one. The separation disappears. What was missing from the training or from that experience in all those years, was my ability or interest in connecting with people in their entire humanity.

ANDREA: What's the difference between connecting with someone in the way you just described and "in their entire humanity"?

DIANA: In the last nine years, since I've been away from that particular style of training, I've been more accepting of people, more understanding of what life is like "off the mat."

During the aikido years, I was most interested in people when we were training or meditating. I was interested in exploring that underground power together. In the years since, I've been coming up aboveground and saying, "Hey, gee, people live and work and play in life, not only train." It has to do with owning up to my own humanity and vulnerability.

ANDREA: What were you hoping to find in that time?

DIANA: I don't know if I hoped to find anything. I would check in with myself every six months and say, "Am I doing what I want to be doing? Am I living where I want to be living? Is this how I want to spend my days and my evenings?"

The answer was always, "Yes."

I never thought I would stay that long. When I first went to Mountain View, I thought it would be about six months. I would just kind of re-up, and it evolved into many years. I wasn't looking for anything. I was just training.

You might say, "Training for what?"

I thought I was training for life, I guess.

On the mat, *uke* represents energy coming toward me, anything I have to deal with: job, boss, spouse, kids, lover, whatever. (Now, I might say, "the other part of myself.") On the mat, in a safe arena for playing out how I deal with energy in the world, I got to practice dealing with that energy. I practiced blending with my boss and blowing it, but it didn't matter because I was not at work, I was only on the mat.

When I got off the mat—I talk about this with nine years of being off the aikido mat—I learned that there are other "mats."

In some ways, the aikido mat was more fun than the world mat. Being out of flow didn't have the consequences that being out of flow in a relationship might have, or in a business. In aikido, you get up and try again, you get another chance. Sometimes in life, that second chance doesn't come so easily.

ANDREA: When you left, did you sense that your aikido time was over?

DIANA: I chose to spend time with my father who was approaching his death. That involved my choosing to leave the training.

Have you ever done a practice where you are sitting on a chair and someone's behind you pressing down on your shoulders, and you have to stand up?

ANDREA: No.

DIANA: Someone is standing, usually on something, and they're putting pressure straight down on your shoulders. If you try and stand straight up against that pressure, it's impossible. But if you let yourself drop down into your belly and into your feet and into an elevator shaft beneath the floor and ride up with it, suddenly you can stand. And it's almost like you're bringing them up with you, your power is so great.

When Bob asked me why I was leaving, I said, "It's like the sit/stand practice. There's a time when you know that's the time to stand."

It felt like the right timing. I made a commitment to go east for a year. I thought I was coming back. It wasn't an act of separation from California.

A year after I left, I was in Manhattan, dealing with the corporate world. I discovered that I had to start all over as a "white belt." The tools I had learned were valid, but it's a different kind of training. It gave me a lot of respect for other people and other paths. My arrogance had led me to believe that my path was by far the best thing going.

Did the aikido training prepare me? Absolutely. It gave me a context to experience this new mat in.

In New York, I did a little bit of training in the Bond Street *dojo*, but it was different for me. I just wasn't drawn into it. I was doing other things, and dealing with a new relationship with Richard. Probably the reason I didn't go often is they spent a lot of the warm-up time doing forward rolls!

ANDREA: What did you do for work?

DIANA: I created a new career. I didn't want to do massage when I got to New York. I thought, "Hey, I'm in New York City. I lived in California from 1968 to 1982. I ought to drop in to this unknown world of the Executive and see what it's like." I wanted to see what this world was and how I could play in it.

I got introduced to computers. I have worked for the last eight years as a person who trains people how to use computers. I got back into teaching people about awareness a couple of years ago, because, while the computer work was nice, I thought that my ability to help people grasp the joy that's inside themselves, and their connection with source is more valuable and more needed. I created two workshops called, "Metaphysical Moments," and "The Art of Happiness."

Happiness is not an ethereal thing. It doesn't just waft your way, and you either have it or not depending how the wind is blowing. It's something that you have to take charge of in your life. You're pro-active—able to respond to the world in a way that creates joy for you or makes you miserable. Sorrow and loss do occur within it. Happiness isn't necessarily a giddy, ha-ha thing. It's this inner sense of who I am. My workshops provide body awareness and energy awareness as the main tools, and I teach them well. And now, there's the moving meditation, t'ai chi chih.

A few years ago, when I first experienced it, I thought, "These are really simple movements, but they're kind of neat." I did them for a while, then I stopped.

I got back into it, and taught it to my husband. We started doing them together. I discovered through his experience that here was something for people who are not going to study aikido or a deep meditation discipline.

We used to ask the question years ago, "How much body awareness do you need? How much is enough?" We never quite knew. We knew that aikido must not be the only way to tap these deeper sources and powers. Suddenly, I had this tool called t'ai chi chih, "Joy Through Movement" that can teach people energy awareness. And it's easy.

ANDREA: When I see the people in the parks moving harmoniously in slow motion, is that what I'm seeing?

DIANA: Yes, you are seeing t'ai chi, probably a variety of forms of it. T'ai chi chih was created by a Western man who was teaching the traditional t'ai chi chuan. His system is very easy to learn, and easy to practice. It utilizes the basic yin/yang principles of t'ai chi and makes it available to people who might not otherwise dedicate themselves to studying the more complicated forms, which take a long time to learn. Instead of the traditional 108 sequential moves, t'ai chi chih consists of only twenty slow movements, each done repetitively, and an alternation of movement with stillness. The moves are simple and they're extraordinary. I see people quickly slip into a universal state of mind, even at the first class.

When I was doing aikido, I thought that t'ai chi was very beautiful. I felt t'ai chi was very similar to aikido, but that aikido was preferable because it gave me another person, a body to work against, so it wasn't a question of just flowing the energy out through my hand, it's flowing the energy out through my hand with somebody hanging onto it. I was always asking to be tested.

In t'ai chi chih, I have to trust my own sense of flow. No one is "testing" me, putting pressure on me. Now I think it's fine to do something that makes me feel absolutely wonderful, because I see that in normal daily life, in relationships, and in marriage, I'm being tested all the time.

It's not necessary to provide people with another chance to be tested. I provide them with a practice that helps them to alter their state of mind, to really be in themselves, and to feel their connection to the earth—or whatever it is they want to feel connected to. Then they can take that out to whatever mat they're working on.

ANDREA: You said early on, "I am not a jock." But much of what you talk about that's meaningful for you involves a physical connection.

DIANA: I am a body awareness junkie. For example, now, I stretch myself by doing what for me is the equivalent of a *sutemi.* On the beach, there are chunks of concrete from a road and a foundation that got torn away by a storm. It feels a little like California because the surf comes up against rocks.

Anyway, there's also an old concrete pier that's a little more than a foot wide and goes out about seventy-five feet into the Gulf.

Some people have no problem walking back and forth on that pier. They go out and fish there. I walk out there, and I get nervous. These thoughts come: "I'm going to get blown over. I'm going to slip." So, I decided to do t'ai chi chih there. There's nothing around me but water on all three sides. I go all the way out to the edge.

I very slowly do some t'ai chi chih. I keep relaxing and playing with the rush that comes from being out there. I guess it's physical, but I'm focussing on my awareness within my body.

It is a paradox. I'm not into cardiovascular exercise. When I say I'm not a jock, that's what I mean. I'm rarely motivated to work out. I know it sounds crazy since I trained in aikido seven times a week for twelve years.

ANDREA: What draws you forward?

DIANA: I'm drawn to those moments of connection, to experiencing the all that we can be, the real human potential, and the mystery. I'm drawn to those experiences that allow that mystery to manifest in me and through me.

I play with it through relationship right now. I choose in my relationship to take the extra step it might take to get beyond a first reaction, to get back to a place of oneness and wholeness with each other where we can experience the mystery, experience the joy of our connection, and then deal with whatever the issues are.

Everyone has their own pier to do t'ai chi out on the end of. Everyone has something that to somebody else is no big deal. Probably, people walk out on that pier, who, if I said, "Do a headstand and then stand on your hands," would be able to do it. Many people don't get nervous out there, but I do. So, I play with it.

Like in aikido, for some people, being *nage* and being the one who kind of directs the show is more challenging than being *uke*. For others, it's the reverse.

ANDREA: Did getting your black belt make you feel physically safe in the world?

DIANA: No. But, I went through a period when people would say, "Does this mean that you can take care of yourself if you're in trouble?" I used to wonder. Then I was afraid that my wondering would draw me into a situation where I'd have to prove it, so I decided that I didn't need that kind of proof. It was not important to me to know whether anything I had learned on the mat was ever going to be useful to me in a physical situation. Thank you very much, I don't need that lesson.

So, I don't know. They say that the true success of a martial artist is never having to be in a fight. I have never been in a fight. Maybe I'm a successful martial artist. I didn't see my training as having anything to do with physical safety. I've never sensed the universe was a scary place. But, the training and awareness make me less likely to be a victim in any situation.

With aikido training, I don't walk like a victim. I sense my surroundings and feel my feet on the ground. When I walk through the world, I know who I am. In that way, it's made the world safer. This is the sense of self that I hope to give people with t'ai chi chih.

ANDREA: It sounds like t'ai chi chih gives you the meat of it.

DIANA: It gives me the heart of it. People used to make fun of Bob's students a lot. We would spend extra time getting ready to do a technique. We were very comfortable and enjoyed that process of, "OK, I'm going to stand here, and I'm asking you to not attack me until I have a sense that I'm in this larger flow and that I'm ready." For me, t'ai chi chih is a lot like just hanging out in that place. Going forward and asking for the attack is what the rest of life is about.

ANDREA: What do you do with all you learned?

DIANA: I share it. I keep, as often as possible, returning to that place of connection. In whatever I'm doing, respect that very real part of me. It's the part of everyone that makes us alive.

Our challenge on earth is to experience connection, while we're in a state of separation. As human beings, we are always separate, physically. As spirit, that separation is not there. But we are human beings, and we are here.

What do I do with it besides enjoy it? It's there to be touched, dipped into, and brought into all aspects of life. I take it into the world. What is a successful person? What do I want my world to look like? Right now, Richard and I have created a life near the beach, as we set out to do. What does this mean to us? What will we create here?

ANDREA: Is there anything else that you want to say about the heart of the matter?

DIANA: I don't know if I've mellowed, or if I see that life is longer than maybe I first thought it was. More moments could be spent focusing on the joy of the moment, on looking around and being part of the world. Certainly, growth comes from having a partner who will call me on my weaknesses, test me, and mirror for me. Yet that can be balanced with the joy and the aliveness of being alive.

ANDREA: What things do you do to support that sense of aliveness?

DIANA: My t'ai chi chih practice. My relationship. My teaching. It's kind of inbred in me. That's what I got from all those years.

As I'm talking to you, I'm sort of stretched out here on the glider, and my feet are draped over another chair. It's gotten a little cooler so they've been moving around looking for warmth.

As I was talking, I could feel myself connecting with my feet. My choice in looking for words is not to go off into my head, but to find them in my feet. To trust that if I can drop into my own center, if I can let go to my own heart, what I say will be appropriate and will really express what I mean.

Today I speak often of love. There really isn't anything else. Love is how I now often label the energy, the *chi*, the *ki*. Body awareness is letting love through my body, experiencing it in my toes, my thighs, my heart, my fingertips, my breath, and my cells. Love with no object, not even a subject. Love with no thought of love, no thoughts at all, only that experience that each of us can only know for ourselves. It is this that I share with others.

As we were finishing up talking on the phone, she said, "Well I guess I better get on my bike and go check out the sunset." In a later note she wrote, "Summer drones on here, the mosquitos try to drive us behind screens at night. Still, the sunsets are forever and the horizon is distant. Way out where it should be. Siesta Key has some kind of magic."

Cyndy Hayashi-Clark

Born in San Francisco, California, in 1954, CYNDY HAYASHI-CLARK grew up in the Bay Area. She attended City College and studied radiologic technology. She also studied aikido in Japan in the early 1980s and has trained in the United States for many years. Her main aikido teachers have been Bill Witt, Saito Sensei, Frank Doran, Frank McGouirk, Saotome Sensei, and Hiroshi Ikeda. Cyndy is the principal x-ray technologist at a research center for osteoporosis in San Francisco. She also teaches aikido. She is married and lives in Redwood City, California.

When I arrived at Cyndy's house, I walked up the pathway past a very wild and weedy front lawn. Throughout the interview, our pauses were punctuated by the faint tinkle of wind chimes, the music of her finches singing in the kitchen, and the buzz of her husband John's applying the weed-whacker.

Periodically, this young man, with a beautiful English accent and a head of pure white hair, would poke his head in the door for one reason or another. A large Akita puppy would bound in and out, accidentally unplugging the tape recorder and joyfully sticking his head in on our conversation. Cyndy responded to all interruptions with equanimity.

She has been training for twelve years. She rose in the ranks remarkably fast, getting her shodan *in her first two years of training and her* nidan *less than two years after that. She holds a fourth degree black belt. In college Cyndy had played badminton competitively. She started doing aikido after she finished school.*

CYNDY: As I shifted from badminton, a competitive art, to aikido, a noncompetitive art, I wondered, "How do they get better if they don't compete? How do I excel here physically? What happens in the process?" I asked my teacher, "We don't do competitions, and you're not supposed to compete with your partner. How do you gauge if you're getting better?"

He said, "I don't think you should worry about that. Just come and train. You'll find out. Later on, you'll thank me for this. Just be comfortable with not knowing." It was getting a little boring. I kept thinking, "There has to be an answer to all of this. It's just not coming in here every day and doing the same move over and over." I was going, "Hum, hum, hum. Everything's the same." That's when he told me, "You just have to switch your awareness into other things." And it became interesting for me. I saw the competition was with myself more than anybody else. It's all internal. That's why I'm constantly pushing myself now on a higher level to find what there is for me to learn from day to day. I always find something.

ANDREA: Have you ever had to use your aikido on the street?

CYNDY: When I was a year and a half into the training, I was attacked by two young black men who were much bigger and taller than me. It was a rear attack, and I was so tired that I wasn't aware of what was happening around me, which is something that you're not supposed to do. But after a full day of work, I was tired. As I got off the bus, I was muddling over, "Should I go to class and do martial arts, or should I go home and go to bed?"

My training really took over for me. I don't remember making decisions about the way I moved. I looked, and I knew it wasn't anybody I knew. I knew it was an attack. I just dealt with it, and did not get hurt. One of them grabbed me from behind in a "bear hug" and I used a hip throw, the other came in from the side and I kicked him in the stomach. My purse was taken, but that was the least of my worries. In that area, a two-against-one situation usually results in a beating and a rape. They got up, grabbed my purse, and started running.

At first, I felt relieved. Then I thought, "They have my purse." I ran after them into the housing project. That's when my defenses came up again. I thought, "This is asking for it."

So, I went home. I didn't live too far away. I called the police. When they came out, one said, "What martial art do you do?" He didn't even ask me anything about how I was. Obviously, I was OK.

I asked, "How do you know I do that?"

He said, "All of the other three women who were attacked today by the same two men are in the hospital, and they've been beaten. One has a broken hip. They're all female Asians. You're the only one who's not hurt, not scratched. You must do something." I told them where I studied.

He said, "Did you break anything on them?"

I said, "No. Why would I want to do that?"

They said, "Because you would have done us a favor. If we catch them, we have to put them in jail, and they usually get out the next day. If you defend yourself and hurt them, that would perhaps make them think twice. They've really hurt three other women."

I thought about it, and I said, "I don't know how to hurt anybody." I went back to my teacher, Bill Witt, and I said, "This is what happened."

He said, "I'm real happy that you're safe. You know, the availability to hurt somebody is always there, and I can show you where those areas are."

We duplicated everything. He showed me how to break stuff. He tempered it and said, "But the fact is that you didn't hurt them. You made an unconscious decision because you didn't know how to make a conscious one. I think that says a lot for your training. Now if they really came in after you, after they had the purse, I would hope that you'd use these tactics because you would have to save yourself."

After that—it didn't affect me like I was shaking or anything—but the things he said to me told me that this was an art that would make me grow personally very strong. More than learning how to hurt anybody in a defensive situation, that's what I wanted to do. I wanted to be like Bill. I wanted to be a real strong person.

"What is a strong person?" is always a big issue with martial arts. What is strong? For me, strong means having a good sense of self,

knowing who I am and what I'm capable of—not how effective I can be physically on the mat, or how much I can really kick butt or win in any situation but how my character holds up against a barrage of things.

After talking the attack over with Bill, I began to look at all of the things that were presented in the class. Not just copying the technique physically, but also looking at the way it affected the other person. The training can be rigorous, but how does it apply to helping the other person as well? It became more complicated. I started seeing the relationship in everything.

It's an incredible responsibility. And as I became more and more advanced, I realized how much more I needed to know, in order to control the situation. If you're just learning techniques, that's fine. It's all very simple. But as I became more and more advanced, I realized how powerful those techniques are: how they can hurt, and also how they can not hurt.

Soon after the multiple attack that I had, I decided to go to Japan for two months. When I came back, because I loved the training, I decided to return immediately. I quit my job and went for seven more months. In those seven months, I trained and I really wanted to be there. Because of that, after six months in Japan, my teacher said, "Tell me when you want to go up for your test."

I said "Well, what test exactly?"

He said, "*Shodan.*"

I said, "You made a mistake. I'm just a second *kyu*. I have to go for first *kyu* first."

Everyone looked at me, and someone said, "You don't tell Sensei what rank you're going for. You just take it."

I thought, "Oh, that's right. I'm in Japan. I'm sorry." I said, "OK. But I've only been trained for less than two years."

He said, "Oh, you're really fast. That's good."

I said, "I guess it was meant to be. I guess I'll do it."

I went to a fairly strict school. I was in a very simple state of existence where I just trained, ate, and slept. As a third-generation Japanese American, I had never gotten a sense of what Japan truly was like. For me to go back was a very enlightening experience.

I saw things inside of me that were there from birth, that my mother and father had given me. I didn't know how to describe those qualities, but they were very apparent in the Japanese people. When I went there, my teachers said, "You don't speak Japanese very well." And I didn't. They continued, "But you have the sense of a Japanese woman. You have that feeling. It's all there. The qualities are there. But when you open your mouth, it's like we don't know where you're from." That brought to my attention what I had and what I didn't have as far as Japanese culture is concerned.

I made a concerted effort to study and discover what they see in a Japanese woman that I didn't have. And did I want that or not? I consciously decided what to retain and what to throw out. It helped me in the *dojo*, and it helped me in life to know that.

ANDREA: What did you want to retain?

CYNDY: A Japanese woman has a very nurturing spirit. They are wonderful mothers. They are extremely compassionate. The Japanese generally saw in American women a hardness that they didn't say was bad, but they did say was just different, a little harsh. There's a different sense of the person if they're Western. I know I had that when I went there.

One of my girlfriends was really insulted when a Japanese man came up to us at a party and said, "Both of you should be in the kitchen, cleaning. You're not supposed to be out here." I thought, "He's right." And I just went and I started washing dishes, and cleaning up. She sat on the bench, and said, "I am absolutely not moving. I am not going to do this." It was a feminist point of view. I thought, "Well, she can do that. She chooses to do that." But then, the Japanese man judged her, and said, "She's definitely Western." That affected the way they related to her from then on. I was in the kitchen. They came in, and they thanked me for doing that. They said—it was kind of demeaning in a way—"You're doing what a good Japanese woman should do. You're in there, cleaning." At first I thought, "I really hate this." But afterwards, they knew I wanted to learn. The wife of one of my teachers, Saito Sensei, taught me how to cut vegetables, and do different things. She invited me to pick things out of her garden. I sensed they really wanted to show me the right way to do that stuff. My friend Marge eventually understood that too. Later, she lived there for a long time with her husband and got a true sense of Japan and the culture.

I realized that in order to learn what the Japanese people had to offer, I had to be like them. I looked like them. They expected me to be a Japanese woman. So I indulged them, and I did what they said. I said, "OK, that's fine." Because, big deal if I have to wash dishes while there's a party going on. I have a whole lifetime of parties. I'm only going to be in Japan for a short period. While I'm here, I can do that and not feel bad about it. I didn't think it was going to affect me in any way. It opened up a doorway for me to learn nothing is demeaning.

ANDREA: What was your transition like from being the student to being the teacher?

CYNDY: It was uncomfortable. There were so many highly ranked people in Japan. A teacher is considered fourth degree or above. It's ridiculous for a *shodan* to think of being a teacher. Here in America, it's different. A person who gets a black belt wants to open a school right away, as if they have the key to knowledge. When I was asked to teach a beginner's class, when I had just returned from Japan and gotten my black belt, it was difficult for me to say, "Yes." I thought, "*Shodan* means beginner level. That means I have the tools to learn. That doesn't mean that I have the knowledge to teach."

People say you have to be fourth degree and above to be a professional teacher, not because they're trying to control you and the money and the ranking system, but because they realize how much you can affect an individual by the way you guide them. Being an aikido teacher, a lot of times you change people simply by saying, "Look up," or, "Open up here. Just stand up, chest out, look up. Be more confident in your posture." As I teach them, I might be changing a lot of internal things that I am totally unaware of. I have to recognize that and be responsible. If I change something, and emotionally something comes out of them, a crisis of some kind, they must not be left alone to deal with that. They have to have somebody there to tell them it's OK. If I don't know to recognize this, then I'm not there for them. Then I can do damage.

As a teacher, now, I train people, learn where their limitations are, and then take them just a little step beyond that so that they learn how to be on the edge physically and emotionally and have a healthy experience there. That's a very delicate thing to do.

ANDREA: How does it benefit people?

CYNDY: If you're always in a safe place, you never know what you're capable of doing. For many people, that's OK. If I read in a student that they want to hang out at a certain level, then I let them be. But if I see a student who is actively trying to be on an edge and progress, then I help them walk to the edge. I have them stay there for a short period of time until I feel it's time for them to back off a bit.

I have to really be careful. If I let my own ego take over, I'm controlling a person. I can affect their life drastically if I don't know what I'm doing. When I look at a person, and I know that I'm pushing them beyond a certain limit, in a way I'm gambling with their life. If it doesn't go well and something happens, I'm responsible for helping them get back into a healthy state. I always make this commitment to myself: whatever I do with a person, if it doesn't work out well, then I'll apologize to them or talk to them. Or I'll help them back to where they are more comfortable.

Luckily, I haven't had that situation happen. With most of the people who've trained, I've had very positive experiences with them. Very powerful, moving things, too.

Recently I trained a woman for her first black belt. She's a very graceful, giving, physical person. A very strong woman. I would train her in free style. Three-person attack, no problem. As soon as four came in, she totally lost it. Something in that number four set something off in her. I noted other little things in her training. She had a tendency to push people away from her. One day, we had an especially hard training for her. I ran her right into the floor, and then I gave her a four-person free-style attack on top of that. I gambled that she would be strong enough to take that type of training.

She started to cry. I could tell that she was right on the edge of something major. After the class, I brought her into the dressing room privately, and I asked her, "What is it about four people? What is the problem?" She said, "I was raped by four men. There's something about having four people running around me. I get scared." I asked her, "Do you want me to stop doing four people? Because if you do, I will. But, I have a sense that you really need to do this.

The people out there are friends. They've trained with you for years. They want only to do what's good and healing for you. And I will always be there to guide it. You will never be in any danger. Here you can face that dragon and kill it, get rid of it." She said, "Yes. I would like to do that. Help me."

In *randori*, the multiple attack, we often blend. Blending is sensing the direction and intensity of the attack and turning to move with it or redirect it. So in receiving the attack, I don't lose the tone of my muscle, but I bring the person in so that I can control them. She positioned her body so that she was trying to hang on to them, grapple, and throw—a lot of work that she didn't need to do. She explained to me that when she was being raped, she was constantly pushing out against the men in that manner. On the mat, that action just solidified the whole thing about fear. So we worked on allowing her arms to move, allowing her lower body to blend and deal with the attackers, and having a sense of centeredness, of calm when she was doing it. We started very slowly and worked her all the way up into a full-scale four-person attack. Her *shodan* test was inspirational. She was really strong. But it took a lot of work to bring her through that moment and other moments in her training. For me, it was a huge growth period. I had not before worked with somebody who'd had that big a trauma.

ANDREA: What were you doing to protect her?

CYNDY: I would position myself so that she could always see me. She had to use her peripheral vision, but everyone does in order to spot, move, and function with four people coming in. I was always there both physically and mentally. I would always stop it if it became too much for her. Also, I was there for her emotionally, anytime she needed me; not just at school, but she could also come over to my house and talk. I always give that to my students. I'm available for them. I'm not just a person on the teaching staff who tells them what to do, and then has nothing to do with them socially.

ANDREA: What does that contribute to a person's training?

CYNDY: I think they realize that teachers are people. That's important. Martial arts instructors can fall into a trap where they believe that they are holier-than-thou.

That's where I defeat myself in the training. I lose the sense of humanity within myself, of being just like the beginner who walks in the door. I keep in touch with the people who are brand-new, coming up in the ranks. It puts it right in front of my face: "This is what I need to do, too—be just like them with a beginner's mind."

ANDREA: Is it effective to say what is on your mind in your teaching?

CYNDY: I use a direct, gutsy type of talking. It works wonders. Rather than beating around the bush, for instance, if I see someone hurting another person on the mat, I say, "Why are you dumping her on her ass like that? Why are you being so brutal?" Or, "Are you intending to be cruel, or am I just dreaming?"

They look at me, and they say, "Me? Cruel?"

"Yes." And then I look at the other person, and say, "Is he being cruel to you?"

"Well, kind of."

I say, "Kind of yes, or kind of no?" I demand that directness from them on the mat. It takes all of the responsibility right back into their field. Instead of acting the teacher and saying, "Don't do that," I say, "Why are you doing that?" And, "Isn't he doing that to you?" Or, "How do you feel? Do you like that?"

If they say, "Yes, I like it," then I say, "I have to talk to you about that. Because it's very self-destructive. Sitting there and taking pain is detrimental to your health." In our *dojo*, if you want to "go ballistic," the upper right-hand corner of the mat is yours. Going ballistic is agreeing with your other partners to train at a high intensity that tests your limits. If you want a lower intensity of training, the rest of the mat is yours.

Having a sense of humor on the mat is extremely important. To have lightness about something as serious as a martial art is imperative. With the person who will be responding to a multiple attack on the mat, I always use the analogy of, "Bowling ball, egg, and feather. You have to juggle all of these different ranks. You figure out who the bowling ball is. It's usually the guy with the *hakama* and black belt on. Figure out who the egg is. Figure out who the feather is." They always get it. They laugh about it, and it sticks with them.

ANDREA: How did you get your *nidan*?

CYNDY: About two years after I returned from Japan, my teachers said, "We want you to go for your second degree." I said, "Why?" And they said, "Because you've trained second degrees for their test. It's unfair for you to be training second degrees, and not be a second degree yourself." I told Frank Doran, my teacher, "I don't feel ready to do a *nidan* exam." He jokingly said, "Well you can always go back and be a first *kyu.*" There was no way out. I said, "I'll take the *nidan.*"

After watching my test, Saotome Sensei, another of my teachers said, "You're too male, too masculine. You make such hard faces for a pretty woman." I was taken aback. I was somewhat insulted, too. I thought, "I'm trying to do a martial art. I don't know what to think about this guy. He's a master, but what does he mean that I should be more feminine? That's really weird." I was angry. I was probably more confused than anything. When I went into third degree, I realized what he was saying, and I was so thankful that he said it to me.

He really was looking at me, and saying, "She has the potential to be a good martial artist, and yet she's being something that she's not. She's not being herself." When I started to train more intently with Frank Doran, he taught me a sense of self.

I tried to watch Frank a lot. He said, "You can always watch me. You can always try to copy me. But you'll never be Frank Doran. You'll always be Cyndy Hayashi. So, why don't you look for her and see where she is? Take what you want from each teacher, but always retain who you are. In that sense, whatever we give you becomes yours." As the years went by, I started to notice that there's a specific way that I move. There is a way that I look at things and apply them. I went from being more angular and applying more strength in my technique, to being very soft, very flowing, and yet martially still correct in my stance and in the way I applied my techniques.

I have the personal power to inflict a very strong hold. I can do a good punch. I can do a good kick. But I don't have to. I can opt for a softer, more graceful way of doing things. If necessary, the harsh response is there if I need it. Because of that, I look completely different now. And I am what Saotome Sensei said: very feminine on the mat. A lot of people have commented that I am physically very strong, and yet I don't apply that on the mat. My training is very soft. I have learned that internal strength and skill need not be demonstrated outwardly with macho stances.

ANDREA: How do you combine femininity and effectiveness?

CYNDY: By being graceful and yet soft. I pin somebody, have the right position, but am not straining to hold him down. I'm very confident that my body position will be correct. I try to be as natural as possible. I don't take up false stances. I don't have extraneous movements, flourishes at the end. Whatever is needed, I do.

I have a sense of knowing exactly what I can do. And I know that my training has great depth, because I've had experiences a lot of people don't normally have the chance to have. I went to Japan and trained every day. I train almost every day in America. I've done that for quite a number of years.

ANDREA: Do you have the sense that there are other paths not taken that you would like to take? How do you include them?

CYNDY: Part of my path in being a teacher is to know not just the way of martial arts, of defense, but also the way of healing. Just like if you want to know nonviolence, you have to have an understanding of violence. Learning body work has been important for me. I need to have a sense of how my hands can be healing hands.

ANDREA: Where do you see that taking you?

CYNDY: I always go into things at a gut level. I go into this not knowing where it's going to lead me, but as long as I feel good about it, I'm going to continue to do it.

ANDREA: What does aikido mean to you?

CYNDY: Aikido is more than just a self-defense. It's much, much deeper. It's a philosophy of life. My whole sense of aikido is like a universal compassion. It's knowing that no matter how bad somebody may appear, there's always some little bit of good in them—something that is salvageable. If I can go out and touch that person in some way, then perhaps I help him into a better light. For me, that's what aikido is. I train on a mat, go to a seminar. I always run into different personalities on the mat. They all have their own little trips they're going through. For me, to be just right there and very empty and just do what I do, and sense what's going on in that end and work with it, that's the art. In that way, it's like water. It's constantly changing. Doing that in my hospital work is the same thing.

ANDREA: How do you apply that philosophy in your work?

CYNDY: I work with doctors, and with business people. They come in and everything they do is a "priority." Then another person comes in. They're priority. I put that all into perspective and let them know, "This is the way that it is: your work will be done in time, with whatever else is going on, unless it gets prioritized differently. That's the way you have to accept it."

A lot of times doctors have an ivory-tower attitude, "Well, I'm Joe Schmoe, and I'm like one of the big guys in osteoporosis, and I say it goes this way." I just have to deal with them on a very open level, just like the mat. If they come in with an attack, and I have a response, I stick to that response. Once they commit to something, there has to be one response, and that's it. I do constant verbal fencing at work. A lot of times, the way I present myself physically when I get introduced to somebody has a great bearing on the way they approach me.

ANDREA: How do you present yourself to be most effective?

CYNDY: I'm very outgoing. As soon as somebody enters my area, I give them the sense that I am in control, and I know exactly what to do in my area. If they want to learn what we do, they'll learn it my way. I will be accommodating in every way I can to them, but they cannot abuse their privileges when they're in my area.

ANDREA: Before you did aikido, what was your feeling about your personal space or your work space?

CYNDY: I was abused. I used to be a very receptive person. I was very shy. I would not dare to think of changing anything. I was more like a sheep than I was one of the pack dogs out there leading them around. My aikido training helped me get a sense of self so that I could feel really comfortable about what I was doing. I know I can do this job, and I do it well. I do it better than almost anybody in the nation, and lots of people come out here to study from us, to learn our techniques. Therefore, in order for me to teach them, I have to have a sense of confidence about what I do.

ANDREA: How do you explain how effective you are?

CYNDY: When I have passion for what I do, then I can do anything. Anybody can do anything if they have passion for it. The passion comes from very deep inside. It stems from a desire to grow and learn. It comes from my desire to make a small but meaningful imprint on this earth.

ANDREA: Does your husband do aikido?

CYNDY: Yes. I always had a sense that I would end up with some-body in aikido. Otherwise, he'd be a widower. It's always *dojo, dojo, dojo.* John is one of the first men who ever physically pushed me on the mat. He has incredible internal power.

I never had anyone throw me as hard as he did, without know-ing who I was. At first, it ticked me off. And then I thought, "OK, it's time to go totally ballistic on this boy." I always have a sense of appropriateness on the mat. I thought, "OK, my face just got mashed into the mat, and it's time to have some fun." I know how hard I could push somebody. We really went at it.

Frank came by and watched. I think he was afraid we were hav-ing a fight on the mat. But we weren't. Actually it was quite clean, pure training. It was martial arts in essence. At the end of it, I thought, "That was really intense. It was very purifying for me to be able just to go at it, and not worry about hurting somebody." We got to talking and chatting. He's a very shy man, actually. He's very English. We went on a walk. After the third day of the summer retreat, where we were training, he said, "Well, I'd like to see you some more after this. And I have a feeling I'll be seeing you often."

I said, "You live down in L.A. It's really not very reasonable. Long-distance relationships do not work."

He said, "Well, things may change." It was funny. He really touched me. I can always tell when somebody's coming from their heart. When he said, "I will be seeing you," I believed him. He went off to do a camp down in L.A. He left to come back and stay with me up in San Francisco. He brought me a commemorative T-shirt. It was a very fast relationship. We just decided to live together, and he brought everything up from L.A. I told him the pitfalls of living with me right out front. He said that no matter what, he wanted to be with me because I was the first person he had ever met that was as honest as I was. That's one of my characteristics: whatever I feel, I'll tell you. A lot of times that gets me into trouble because I'll say things that may be borderline rude. I've lived with the consequences of that, but I think in the long run, it's a healthier way to be.

Whenever he does not want to train, that's fine. I go ahead and train. He stays at home and walks the dog, or does the laundry, or does his woodworking, or whacks the weeds out in front. When he wants to train, and I don't feel like it, I stay home. That's kind of rare, but I have done that on occasion. I stay home and do what I need to do.

ANDREA: You talked about meeting this man and pulling out the ballistics. You're a short person—what is the power you're bringing forth?

CYNDY: In aikido, depending on the timing and the position, I can take a person much larger than myself and just slam them into the mat. When I met John, I was at peak condition. I could go out there and pound. I was not afraid of taking someone's balance and just slamming them, knowing that he could take the fall. I like training hard. I've never been intimidated by size. I've lived in very poor neighborhoods, and was brought up in a ghetto. Because of that,

I've had to be fairly strong internally. I know that if I'm in a corner, and I need to defend myself, I will do it. And I don't mind. In that sense, death doesn't frighten me as much as losing my personal dignity. I will defend my family or my friends with as much as I have if I need to, and I know I can do that. It doesn't matter to me how much I have to sacrifice myself.

Having that sense makes me more powerful. In fact, that will make the other person back down. They're not willing to take that gamble most of the time.

When I left Cyndy's house, she and her family stood on the front porch to wave good-bye. I said good-bye to Cyndy, to the cheerfully panting dog-beast, and to John, who was covered with a fine coat of the brilliant chlorophyll green of his formerly wild front yard, which now was smooth and well-mannered.

Beth Hall

Darkness has a hunger that's insatiable,
And lightness has a call that's hard to hear.
I wrapped my fear around me like a blanket.
I sailed my ship of safety 'til I sank it.
I'm crawling on your shore.
> —from the tape *Indigo Girls* by the Indigo Girls, as heard on Beth's
> answering machine message.

BETH HALL *grew up in San Diego, California, and started aikido training when she was twelve years old. At the time of the interview she was at a community college, planning to transfer to UC. Now twenty-three, she studies developmental psychology at UC Berkeley. She earned her black belt when she was seventeen. Her first aikido teacher was Wes Levins; her main teachers today are Hoa Newens, Kim Peuser, and Pat Hendricks. I wanted to interview her to learn about the different lessons learned by a woman who had started doing aikido as a child. I was also interested in her experiences with teaching martial arts to children.*

For the interview, Beth and I met in a park which was halfway between her house and my house. She was wearing a black leather motorcycle jacket, purple striped trousers, and blue shoes. It was a cool, damp spring day. While we talked, sitting on cement steps to avoid the damp ground, a blossoming tree shed its pinkish white blossoms on us. By the end of the interview, they were all over the stairs and the ground, like a carpet of magic snow.

Frequently she stood up to demonstrate with her body what she experienced during a moment in her life. Her hands made sweeping gestures, and her torso straightened or slouched, to show that something worked and felt right, or didn't.

ANDREA: Why did you start training?

BETH: In San Diego, in Ocean Beach, where I lived, there were a lot of street-tough kids riding around on bikes. One girl was a real bully, and for some reason, she singled me and my friend out. We walked by the pizza place where everybody hung out, and she saw us. Something about us made her mad. We didn't say anything or do anything. Who knows why kids start a fight?

Anyway, she and her gang followed us up the street. They were shoving us from behind, taunting us, and saying nasty, stupid, seventh-grade-type stuff. Pretty soon they're shoving us even harder, and we're falling down. We were scared. We weren't tough kids.

Finally, she pins my girlfriend on her back. She's straddling her, threatening her, and being really tough, saying, "I'm going to hit you." She took off all her rings and cracked her knuckles. It was over-dramatized, almost like she'd seen it on TV, and wanted to try it out. She didn't actually end up hitting my friend, because she turned on me. I was shoved around and punched in the stomach. Finally we got away from them, ran to somebody's house, and called my dad. In the years to come, I found out more about her. I learned that she was an abused child. Anyway, she was taking out her anger on us.

After that, I was scared of everything. I didn't want to go down to town. My family would go out to dinner, and I would stay home. No matter who I was with, I felt ashamed as well as afraid. I was scared that those people might see me. I felt physically sick.

Then, we found out she was getting transferred to our school. She had gotten kicked out of the other school. I thought I was going to die. She was going to be in one of my classes. By this time, everybody had heard about it. All of our friends were rallying around us, and saying they'd protect us. But I was embarrassed.

I walked home from school that day, and said to my best friend, "I never want to go back to school again." I didn't know what I was going to do. That night, my appendix flared up, and the next day I was in the hospital with an appendectomy. I was out of school for two weeks.

After that, I started school again, and was still intimidated by this girl. My parents could see that I had changed. I was looking like a scared person, not a normal kid. My parents knew Wes Levins, who had a children's aikido program. My mom said, "We want you to take aikido." I resisted it.

They made me do it. They bought me a uniform and drove me to the class. They made sure I went in the door. I hated it. I was always making up excuses to not go. But after about a month, I started to like it. My sisters did it, too. Wes bred Rottweilers, and the Rottweilers had puppies, and we hung out with the puppies a lot. Wes would always give us a ride home. I had a good connection with my teacher.

ANDREA: What happened to the kid who beat you up?

BETH: The next semester at school, I had a class with her. I felt nervous the first day. I was sitting right next to her in the rows thinking, "What do I do if she tries to hit me? If she says something, what do I say?"

My pencil rolled off of my desk, and it rolled up near her. I thought, "Oh my God. I'm going to have to get up and go up there and get my pencil." She bent down, picked up my pencil, turned around with the nicest smile, and gave me the pencil. That sort of melted the ice. I thanked her and I took the pencil.

Gradually over that semester, we got to be friends. She had changed. I think she had a really difficult upbringing, and maybe she had gotten some help. Maybe she had even gone to live with somebody else because her family had broken down. But she was doing better. She was friendly to me and really nice that whole year.

At the end of the year—in high school, you get your school picture taken, and everybody gives each other pictures, and they write something on the back—she gave me a picture of herself. We had never talked about how she had beaten me up. On the back, she wrote something like, "Dear Beth, I'm glad we got to be friends even though it started out a little strange."

People used to say, "Why don't you beat her up? Why don't you get revenge?" It was enough for her to say that. She didn't have to make some big apology to me.

ANDREA: What happened after that?

BETH: That year, Wes and his wife Jenny were tying up loose ends and getting ready to go over to Japan to train. Wes made an arrangement with another teacher to take over the school. Wes and Jenny sold all their stuff, put their car in storage, took their dogs out to the country, and went off to the wilds of Iwama.

The new teacher, Chiba Sensei (a traditional Japanese male aikido teacher) took over the school. With him came a whole entourage of people, Japanese as well as American, who followed him around. I was accustomed to this family relationship with my teacher and his wife and their puppies. The new teacher's *dojo* was hard at first. I was devastated by Wes's leaving. My sisters quit right after Wes left.

At that point, I was a total adolescent, suffering, starting to have ridiculous crushes on boys at school. Just being a teenager was a hard time. Wes wrote to me. He had a sense that I would go places if I stuck with aikido. He also knew that he was coming back someday, and he wanted me as his student. He'd send me postcards, but he'd never say much.

The aikido school moved out to a different part of San Diego because the old space got to be too small. I wrote Wes a letter saying the *dojo* had moved, and I wanted to quit. I was never fully integrated into the adult classes, but I also wasn't part of the children's class anymore. I missed Wes and what we had. I wrote, "I don't think I can keep going. Maybe someday when you come back, I'll start again. School is difficult. It's stupid. A guy broke my heart." And on and on.

I almost hoped he wouldn't write back, and I could quit and forget all about it. He wrote me a letter. I've still got it somewhere. He poured himself into it. It was about ten pages, all in tiny little scrawl, about things that I had never heard from him—about his first teacher and all the suffering and struggling that went on between them, how he had this terrible flu the day before he took his black belt test. He wrote about things that are common to every martial artist—the hardships along the way. He said, "If you can find it in yourself to keep going, then keep going. Don't quit. I know that you have it in you. You may not realize that now, but I know you do. If you can find in yourself what I know is there, then you'll keep doing it." I resented him because it was almost as if he was forcing me to go on. Part of me realized what a long haul it was going to be if I chose to continue, but after that letter, there was no way I could quit. I knew he was right.

Six months later, Wes and Jenny returned to the States. I had been looking forward to his return for so long. When he finally returned, it was a little strange at first. I was the only one of his original students left. So we would go out to Chiba Sensei's *dojo* together, and we would train. It was uncomfortable because Chiba Sensei wanted Wes to be his student, but Wes studied a different style of aikido.

Wes eventually decided to open another school in Ocean Beach. I was part of the whole process of renting out the place, and working with him and his wife. We worked day and night, ripping out the walls, and building the place up. We were working a lot down there at the *dojo*. When we opened up the school, I was the one that showed up. Eventually we got more students. I was the little star because I was only fifteen, but I was a brown belt, his top student, and was helping him teach. It was just the two of us starting with a lot of beginners.

ANDREA: Did that feel like pressure for you?

BETH: At the time, it didn't feel like pressure. Now sometimes I wonder about that. I felt I had to show up. I always wanted to because of my commitment to him and what we were building. We were doing something together. He wasn't making me do something. It was my school, too.

I spent a lot of time down there. We made something out of nothing, taking this empty building and putting down a mat, building an altar for O'Sensei, getting people to come, making flyers, making posters, and doing demos. We got a pretty good group going. We would go to seminars. We were traveling a lot. I'll never forget the first time we came up here. It was 1982. Saito Sensei was coming out here, and we drove up from San Diego, and arrived at the *dojo* he was visiting at 5 AM. We drove all night. That trip was an awakening for me: meeting all of those people and seeing this whole other world of aikido going on up here. That *dojo* was in its heyday. It was an amazing place to be.

I saw Kayla Feder's *nidan* test, and was blown away. I felt not only inspired, but also I wondered, "How can I ever measure up? How am I ever going to get that good?" Those women—Pat Hendricks and Kayla Feder—were like goddesses to me. Nothing could touch them. They could do no wrong. I spent a lot of time with them that week, cruising around, following them around, and doing everything that they said. The whole drive home, Wes and I talked about how we wanted to make the school like theirs, and how we wanted to be like them. He wanted my *shodan* test to be as good as Kayla's *nidan* test. It was a little absurd and we both knew that. I was getting ready for my *shodan.* Pat and Kayla were planning to come down for the test.

ANDREA: What attracted you to them?

BETH: They were the best I'd ever seen, before or since. And I've seen a lot of people train in the United States, Europe, and Japan. They flew. Something about them was so free and so high. Individually, they've retained those qualities.

ANDREA: What do you mean by "flying"?

BETH: Their *ukemi,* their falls. Pat was one of the principal *ukes.* She would take these high, cutting falls like nothing I had ever seen, and they were perfect, every time. It seemed like she never got tired.

Pat and Kayla both came down to train with me for my *shodan.* I was seventeen. It was 1985. They were really working me hard. We'd take the seminars, and we'd be in there hours afterward, long after everybody had gone home exhausted. They were hammering me on my test.

That whole summer, I was getting ready for my *shodan* test. Wes would drop in once in a while, and we would be in class, but he was busy with other things. September rolled around. We'd all been working all week, getting the place cleaned up, painting it, and redoing the mat. Everything had to be impeccable for Saito Sensei, a highly ranked teacher. There was a lot of stress and strain between me and Wes. Pat and Kayla were going to stay with me up at my folks' house when they came down for my test.

They arrived, and it was a whirlwind. That weekend is a blur, even the test itself. By that time, I could do no wrong. They had all spent so much time training with me. I was Wes's top student, and

his first black belt. It was a big day. When it was over and everybody was gone, just Pat, Kayla, and I were in the *dojo*. My parents
had been there and cried and given me flowers and the whole nine
yards. Then everybody had gone. They were all entertaining Sensei. For some reason, the three of us were going to close up.

Usually getting a black belt is very ceremonial. Somebody gives
you a belt and your rank. But everybody had fluttered off with Saito
Sensei, and I was kind of left there with Pat and Kayla. Kayla was
in the dressing room. Pat was folding her *hakama*, and I was sitting
there with her. I remember feeling despondent, and then saying to
her, "I guess nobody's going to give me their black belt."

She said, "Oh, Beth," and took off her belt and gave it to me.
That just—it didn't break my heart—but I wept. Getting that belt
from her was a very big moment in my life. It felt to me as if she
was saying, "Carry on the tradition. Keep that strong training." That
belt was a talisman. I think I slept with it that night. There was a
lot of pain that night. A lot went down with relationships between
people. Everybody was very tense about Saito Sensei being there.
That ended up being one of the best and the worst days.

That belt carried me through. They all left the next day. I went
back to school and brought it to school with me. That belt was the
only thing I had left after this whole whirlwind of activity and the
test. I was really wounded at that time in my life. Looking back,
that was a very, very difficult time. That belt was only a piece of
cloth, but it had belonged to Pat who was really special to me. There
was something more in that act of her giving it to me. Even in years
when I wasn't training very much, and when things were drab and
a drag, I always had that belt.

There was a way in which I was more healed by having that belt
than I was helped by some of the people involved with me at that
time. People weren't there for me so much. I had to be there for
myself, but I had that belt. It's silly. The belt didn't do anything. It's
just a belt.

*In the middle of that year, Beth dropped out of high school. She
moved out of her parents' house, and worked at a health food store*

in Ocean Beach. She spent her spare time watching the sun set, hanging out, and going to reggae shows. After about six months of that, she got back into training. When she was nineteen, she moved into the dojo, getting up at 6 AM to train on the beach.

She moved back to her parents' for awhile, started saving money, and decided to move to the Bay Area. She had gotten her equivalency diploma. She bought a 1965 Dodge van, and her dad helped her build a bed in it and work on it. She made curtains for it, and made it wholly habitable. She drove up to the Bay Area and was there for a short time. Then she went to Oregon for awhile. After a few months, she moved back to the Bay Area, got her own place, started working, and began aikido training again. When the head instructor at the dojo *left, it was taken over by his two top students.*

BETH: When I arrived at the *dojo,* everybody knew me from before, but it was a strange time to be a new person there. In spite of all the changes, I knew I wanted to be there. I knew that no matter who was there teaching, somehow there was going to be something for me.

Hoa Newens, one of the teachers who had taken over the school, took me under his wing. I trained with him more than anybody else. That meant a lot to me. I took my *nidan* test that spring. Kayla took beautiful falls, and made me look good.

That next summer we went to the Aikido Retreat in San Rafael. Hoa was a guest instructor that year. I'd been taking falls for him and training hard all week. I came into class the last morning of the retreat, and I was late. I didn't stretch. I didn't warm up. I blasted right in there and started training. I wasn't even training that hard or fast. But somehow my foot twisted under me all wrong and I broke a couple of bones. I had to get carried off the mat. There was a big weeping scene. Then, I went to the hospital. It seems like you always fall when you're up the highest. I was jamming. Man, I broke that foot, and I thought, "Girl, not only can you not train, you can't even walk."

The lesson in that was I was going too fast. I was stretched to my limit. I had run downhill, and into the *dojo.* I took off my shoes, stepped onto the mat, bowed in by myself, jumped in, and started training. It's different when I bow in and do the warm-ups with the class. Not only is my body prepared, but I'm psychically prepared.

That was a setback. I gained weight. I couldn't even walk. I was miserable. Then I got my cast off and was doing physical therapy. It was hard to start training again after that injury. My foot was always getting stepped on. I never broke it again, but I reinjured it many times. My awareness changed so much. The other day, I was talking with a guy who had stepped on somebody's foot and injured her. I said, "You've got to be really careful."

He said, "Your awareness isn't in your feet, usually."

And I said, "*Your* awareness isn't in *your* feet. My awareness is in my feet. I'm very into how I step, where I step, when I step." It brought me down into that whole part of my body. We are usually in our upper bodies and do things with our shoulders and arms, using upper-body strength. In aikido, you want to get people down into their hips, into their legs, and moving with their whole body. Anyway, that brought my attention way down into what was happening below me, not up here over my head. If I walk far or take a lot of hard falls, it still hurts. When it's cold, I feel it.

ANDREA: What are you doing now?

BETH: This year, I went back to school. In years past, I thought, "Oh, I'm never going to want to go back to school. I'll just have a *dojo.*" But I want more. I want a good education. Now I'm trying to get into the University of California at Berkeley. I'm going to Merritt College, and fulfilling transfer requirements. I'm teaching a lot of children's classes. I teach every day except for Thursday, but I don't get to train as much.

I've been doing aikido for so many years that my self-worth is affected by how much I train. Even though school is important to my future, I don't feel like I'm training enough. I've been accustomed to training a lot. Now I come in, and all these people are training four days a week or more. They're much more integrated into the energy of the school. Sometimes I feel like a stranger there.

ANDREA: When you teach, what do you do to keep the power dynamic clean?

BETH: I remember what it was like in junior high, and some of the kids I teach are experiencing the same feelings. I find myself sometimes getting a little mixed up with them and wanting their approval. A lot of needs and emotions can get confused with the teaching. It's important for me, as a teacher, to be clear about what I'm getting out of it. I can't go in there because I want my students to love me. I have to have some higher goal. It's not only about people and techniques. It's about wanting to create a positive type of energy in the world.

It's easy to have other motives. Motives are very easily confused. There will be times when I do things and I won't even know why I'm doing them. It's really important to keep checking myself. I can't play favorites with the kids. If I start doing that, I'm defeating myself right away. They sense that stuff. In a way, they're checking me by doing that. I'll find myself starting to spend a little extra time or giving a little extra encouragement to one, and I think, "Uh-uh." I've got to make a point to go out and give a little extra to somebody else. But there's more than that. There's only so much that I can do in terms of a technique or an idea or a method. I have to have my own personal clarity, too. Even in my most confused moments, I still have to come across and be there for them as a good teacher.

It's important to not try to get something out of them. It's also important not to be attached to what they do. That's a biggie especially with one of my students. If I get disappointed in him, we're both going to be bummed out. I've got to love him no matter how he shows up. If he shows up defiant and macho, I've got to love him as much as the days when he's helping little Joseph or saying some nice thing out of the side of his mouth as he leaves.

ANDREA: How long have you been teaching the kids I saw?

BETH: I've been teaching this particular group for eight months. I first started teaching children when I was sixteen. I had this idea that I had to be strict, and they should be disciplined. I would try to make them do strict aikido, and they would walk all over me. I realized the more I can let go and let them show up as who they are, the more that they're going to want to do what I want to do. I try to let them do their own thing, and yet still make it clear that there are certain limits. I don't let them leave the mat once I've bowed in, unless there's some obvious emergency. Part of what I'm trying to teach them is to not be at the mercy of their needs all the time. It's learning about commitment in small blocks.

ANDREA: What do you do to maintain serenity in that context?

BETH: If I'm not calm, then they're not going to be calm. If I start to get angry, then they feel that anger. Young people are really sensitive to the moods of adults.

ANDREA: What do you do to prepare yourself?

BETH: I don't come on the mat in a filthy *gi*, or bow in with my *gi* hanging open. I pull myself together when I come into the *dojo,* before I bow. I'm saying, "Here I am. I'm ready." I say good-bye to whatever I left on the street. When I sit down and bow before the altar to O'Sensei, I show my gratitude, but I also ask myself, "How am I going to show up? How am I going to present myself to O'Sensei?" Sometimes I'll get there late. The kids are all already there, and I've got to rush, dress, sit right down, and start. There's something about putting on the uniform. I come out of whatever I was wearing before, and I step into another set of clothes. That's the reason I like the kids to have the uniform. A lot of times they try to wear sweats and I say, "Wear your uniform. Get into this."

ANDREA: Why do you keep going?

BETH: Why do I keep going?
  I would never quit. I've been doing aikido for so long, I could just as soon quit permanently as I could stop eating. But there've been a lot of times when I can't think of a reason to go. Sometimes there are more reasons not to go. I don't want to get into my *gi*, put up my hair, get on the mat, deal with that chronic muscle pull, or

feel my old foot injury. Something more than guilt keeps me going. I've done things out of guilt that I finally ended up quitting. Aikido isn't one of them. I'm getting a lot of inspiration from the kids right now. Teaching them is very fulfilling. They do give me grief, but it's not about whether I did something perfectly or not. Kids look inside. They know whether you're good or not, because they'll like you. They like the way you feel. A lot of adults look for a teacher who's bigger and stronger than them. They want to get pounded. I can't do that. But the kids can all look up to me very easily. I don't have to try to be something big and impressive. I can be this little woman, and do my thing. They're still going to dig me.

Why do I keep going? My reasons seem to change with the seasons. On a bare bones level right now, I keep going because of the kids.

ANDREA: What do you see for yourself? What do you hope for yourself?

BETH: I want to have a school that can offer a traditional aikido (discipline and all that good stuff about a traditional format) but that will be in a less traditional format so that it's open to different kinds of people. Especially to children.

I feel strongly about teaching young people. I can try to teach adults about nonviolence and about conflict resolution, but if they already had a violent upbringing, I can only do so much. If I get a kid and start them young, that's one more person going off into the world with those lessons. That's my hope. That's what I want to do. That's my aikido.

Sarah Wada

Born in Walnut Creek, California, in 1955, Sarah Wada was raised in Massachusetts. She attended college at UC Santa Cruz, and started studying aikido with Jack Wada in 1976. In addition to training in the States, she also studied aikido in Japan for a year at Shingu dojo. She is currently enrolled in the doctoral program in linguistics at UC Santa Cruz. She lives in San Jose with her daughter Jennifer.

Sarah Wada's place was tucked back in a complex of apartments. It was a damp and drizzly day. Sarah greeted me at her door, and invited me inside. When I spoke with Sarah on the phone, her voice was so gentle and so direct that I found myself compelled to soften my tone to match hers. I also found myself able to speak very clearly and without pretense. From our conversations before our meeting, I had been expecting someone small, and quiet almost to the point of meekness. I was surprised to find Sarah to be a tall person, in whose character I saw a harmonious combination of gentleness and fierceness.

We settled in the living room. Through the screen door, a brown flop-eared rabbit on the porch eyed me solemnly during the interview, while birds sang from the other room. A rat walked up the side of its cage, while a cat paced around the room. There were all sorts of books everywhere, books I'd want to have around, and a small piano.

Sarah started studying aikido in school in January 1976. There was also an aikido club which was having winter training. She wanted to watch them, but she wasn't ready to train. She rode her bicycle to the foot of the hill and walked up the hill every morning, to sit and watch class at 6 AM. She admired the teacher, Jack Wada, who spent a lot of time talking about philosophy.

ANDREA: What is the philosophy for you?

SARAH: Frank Doran, one of the teachers in the Bay Area, expressed it the way I like best. He said, "When you're doing aikido, your enemy is not the person that's attacking you. Your enemy is their intent to hurt you. The point of aikido is to neutralize their intent to hurt you without hurting them."

Aikido is soft and receptive without being weak, the curves and spins of it. I like that. I'm not real big on the techniques where you hold someone so their joint is locked. I do like some of the joint techniques: I can feel the other person's body moving and feel connected to them in their center. It's an interesting experience, and it's a good one. Plus, it's a healthy thing to get used to being physically close to people that you may not know well, to let the space around your body be more open to other people. I've enjoyed the fact that I could have other people in my space, and it was OK. It doesn't have to be a big deal if someone's standing close. Other cultures are not necessarily quite so jumpy as we are.

For me, now, I think of aikido as a movement form. I don't want to trivialize it, but I'm not a warrior. It's not a combat art for me. I don't think there's anything wrong with that, but I can see how my style would be irritating to people who want an emphasis in their training, on punches, strikes, and counter-strikes. That's not where my enjoyment of aikido is.

Anyway, while I watched the early morning class, I felt this most incredible energy coming from Jack, and filling the whole *dojo*. I admired him very much. I was amazed by the way things felt watching him teach. Eventually he asked me to go out to breakfast with him. From that point on things got kind of complicated, because we developed a personal relationship which wasn't always harmonious. Mixing training relationships with personal ones is always tricky, particularly when the training relationship is a teacher-student one.

I went away to Seattle that summer. When I got back to Santa Cruz, we sat down and decided to get married. When I had been

away in Seattle—I was at school there taking Japanese—I realized how consistent and kind he'd been. I thought to myself, "All the time, people are complaining about people who won't work at relationships. How could you ask for anybody that could be more consistent and more kindly?" I'd realized that he was somebody I could trust never to walk away from me. I needed that.

For me, aikido training, almost from the beginning, has been affected by our personal relationship. I like aikido a lot, and I miss it now that I'm not training. One of the reasons why I can't train now is there is nobody else who I would want as a teacher, but I don't think it's fair to him or to me to go into the training situation and expect not to have to deal with feelings. I don't think it's fair to ask him to deal with them. I'm not sure that I would want to deal with them either. What I haven't been successful in doing is finding people who I can flow with, and training with them. I'd like that. I've talked with a couple of people, but our schedules are so busy that we haven't had time.

When I was training, I tried to be scrupulous about not having my relationship with the teacher give me license to push ahead of other people, or test when I wasn't ready. I would hold myself back for that reason. When I took my fifth *kyu* test, I was nervous about it. One woman said, "Don't worry. You have connections in high places."

I was shocked. I said, "Oh, I hope you don't think that would make any difference."

However, because I was Jack's wife, I never felt I established a working relationship with any of the teachers in the area. I never felt people respected me or liked me. I wasn't close to anybody when I was training. They'd have big events at the *dojo,* and all these people would come up. The women would seem to me to be really friendly with each other. Maybe they weren't as close as they seemed, but I always felt isolated in a way from people. I'm not used to expecting to connect with people.

ANDREA: What do you think of as your strength?

SARAH: I think I'm honest in a meaningful way. I think that's important and it's something that I don't see very often. A lot of people view honesty as the ability to express what's on the top of their mind without necessarily examining thoroughly to see how much of their own agenda has gone in there.

I'm good at being honest without doing that. Honesty for me does not mean coming up to someone and saying, "This is offensive. You shouldn't do this." It has to do with looking at the situation in a multi-dimensional way and being careful and precise about what I say. I'm also a giving person if people take the time to know me. Most of the people who I talk to say they feel better after they talk to me. I'll say, "If I were you, I'd feel like this . . . " and they say, "Yeah. That's exactly how I feel."

I'm a person who, on the surface, might not seem so friendly because I'm not good at expressing emotions that I don't feel. Superficial friendship doesn't come easily to me. I feel awkward. But the people that I care about, I would do anything for. I'm loyal and loving. For example, my husband and I had a difficult relationship, but I don't bear him any ill will.

Sarah trained for over seven years. After she and Jack married, they went to Japan for almost a year.

SARAH: I liked the style of training at that Japanese *dojo* a lot. It was hard and extreme. One teacher there has a very rough style. He'll knock you around and throw you hard. I was in the *dojo* once, training with him, and he was pushing me down into the mat. I remember thinking, "He wants to wipe the mat with my face. He's going to kill me. Ha!" It struck me as incredibly funny. I didn't get mad. I had a good time training with him and liked him. After that, we got along well. That particular style of martial arts is very martially oriented, very much "live blade." Live blade refers to a sword that has a sharp blade, rather than the dull metal ones sometimes used for sword practice. Live blade training means taking aikido seriously, understanding that you can hurt other people or be hurt yourself if you are not aware and concentrating. It's a very fierce, intense attitude toward training. I remember the teacher standing up in front of the *dojo*, saying, "This is life or death. You have to train hard. You have to be serious. You have to be totally self-sacrificing and dedicated. You have to totally ruin yourself for martial arts. Break your legs and all your bones and totally destroy yourself in the pursuit of this."

ANDREA: It sounds like this didn't scare you.

SARAH: I'm a fairly fierce person by nature. I feel, "Damn straight. If you're going to do something, don't screw around." I don't like it when people are half-assed. That environment is ideal for me. I go in there, and think, "It's nice to see somebody doing something. Enough with these Americans. They just want to play. I don't want to play." I wanted to train, and I liked it.

When we first arrived in Japan, in January, they were having winter training. It was very cold. Sometimes snow would blow into the *dojo* through the small windows at the floor level which were always open. The buildings were never heated. Anyway, every morning at 6 AM we would meet outside the *dojo* and then run over to Kamikura-san, a small mountain shrine nearby. Then we'd go up the steep stone steps to the top and do the Shin-Kokyu, a purification exercise that combines breath, movement, and chanting. Afterward, we'd go down the steps again and run back to the *dojo* in time for class at 6:30 AM. After class, we'd go out for breakfast—coffee and toast usually. Then we were free until evening class, from 7:30 PM to 9 PM. I loved it. It was so exciting to be in Japan, so different. I felt strong and alive.

Eventually, I did get run down, though. I don't think we were eating very well. Meat's expensive. I didn't know good ways of getting protein. Even brown rice is hard to get. You buy brown rice in Japan at the feed store. People say, "Why are you eating that? It's for livestock." We also ate a lot of tofu. Tofu's good for you, but you get sick of eating it all the time. We weren't getting enough food plus everybody wants to go out drinking all the time. We weren't getting enough sleep. I also started to have trouble with my knee, perhaps from doing a lot of knee work on the tatami mats.

That is a harder surface than the foam mats usually used in the United States. In Japan, the floor in the *dojo* is wood with a very thin layer of straw mat, the same as in most of the houses there. It's not all that springy. Tatami is a better training surface than foam mats for a lot of reasons. You feel your bones hitting a little bit more when you hit the mat. The tatami in this country is covered with weird icky vinyl stuff. I hate it. The canvas used in Japan breathes. It does get grubby. I suppose it absorbs sweat, but it's a nice surface to work on.

Shortly after they came back from Japan, in January 1978, Sarah became pregnant. Having received her second kyu *in Japan, she took her first* kyu *test in the U.S. She was pregnant at the time. She took her black belt test when her daughter was about two years old.*

SARAH: Training for my black belt was difficult. Any personal conflict that I had with my husband would surface. He was the head of the *dojo,* was going to put me up for my black belt, and was training me to take that test.

ANDREA: Did the black belt mean anything to you?

SARAH: I was glad when I got it, but my bachelor's degree means a lot more to me. I sweated blood for the B.A. As much as I worked hard for the black belt, it was a natural extension of what I was doing at that time. In Japan, you usually get a black belt if you've been training for a year. So I wasn't that excited; it wasn't this big romantic thing.

ANDREA: Did the gear mean anything to you?

SARAH: Even if I don't train for ten years, I feel that I earned the right to wear the black belt and the *hakama.* I don't like it that traditionally women wear *hakama* when they choose to and men only wear *hakama* when they have their black belts. It makes my *hakama* not as visible an achievement. In Japan, the women wear them all the time.

ANDREA: What was it like to train while you were pregnant?

SARAH: That's when I started to learn to do hard falls. I thought, "If I'm going to use my pregnancy as an excuse not to do hard falls, I'm never going to get to do them." I trained hard. One guy who was very lazy, used to train at the *dojo.* He was a black belt. We were in class one time, and he was looking around for a partner. I swear he wanted to train with me because I was pregnant (by then I was pretty big), and he thought it would be easy. I thought, "Ha!"

In the Japanese *dojo* where we had been, we concentrated on bouncing back up off the floor fast. We would use the fall in a rubbery way. I was down, and I was right back up. I never dropped my energy. I could attack pretty fast, so that's what I was doing. I was all over him. He had to stop. He was breathing hard and said, "I see you had your Wheaties this morning."

I thought, "You thought you were going to have it easy because I was pregnant. Well, think again."

My husband was always pushing me, "Do this. Do that. Train when you're having your period. It doesn't matter if you've got cramps and you feel sick. This woman always trains when she has her period." Push, push, push.

When I was pregnant, I stood up for myself in a big way. I said to myself, "If I'm unhappy, my body will probably produce unhappy chemicals, and those will go into the placenta, and my daughter will feel unhappy energy. So I'm not going to do anything that makes me unhappy because it's for my baby." I was consciously self-indulgent. That was the first time that I didn't let a sense of duty make me do things that I didn't want to do. I was the kind of person who, because I didn't want to do something, would force myself to do it.

ANDREA: Did that sense of limits or knowing carry over?

SARAH: Not really. I trained almost up until my daughter was born. She was born strong and healthy. But after my daughter was born, I was trying to do everything again. When the baby was growing inside of me, it was a presence that developed so gradually that I wasn't aware of it. Every day, it was a little bit more, but it grew so slowly. Gradually, she had been taking more and more energy. But when she was born, she was completely out of my system. I thought, "Wow, I got my body back. This is great." I had so much energy. Immediately, I tried to do everything: train in three classes, get three hours of sleep, clean the entire *dojo*, and cook. I got sick. I was in the hospital within six months of her birth. I think if I had mellowed out after she was born, that wouldn't have happened.

I planned to have her in the *dojo*. There was some concern about what would happen if I was in labor, and there was supposed to be a class? However, everything worked out OK. My water broke at five in the morning, and Jennifer was born in the *dojo* around five o'clock in the afternoon the same day. There was class that night at seven. It didn't interrupt the *dojo* schedule at all. It was nice. And everyone said that the *dojo* felt really nice. Have you been in that *dojo*?

ANDREA: It's a big barn of a place?

SARAH: Yes. I always liked the feeling of that building. I would walk in and like how it felt. But when I lived there for so long, the impact of it diminished. We all lived there until my daughter was eight. There was no kitchen. I cooked on a hot plate. I carried water everyplace. I had to carry the dishes into the men's bathroom, which was the only place where we had hot water to wash. I thought, "We were living in Japan with no hot running water and no indoor plumbing, we had a more convenient and happy lifestyle than we have in this stupid *dojo*. I'm walking up and down the stairs with dishes, we have no refrigerator." It was so silly. I'm the kind of person who wants to putter around the house and cook dinner. It was frustrating.

Living in the *dojo* can really give you a strange feeling of isolation, because even though people are there all the time, and you see people every day, they haven't come to see you and you rarely see them anywhere else. So there are always people around, but it's very easy to feel lonely.

Sarah stopped training around 1980 when her eighteen-year-old sister was killed in a car accident. Sarah's younger sister was a lot like her. They had both been ambivalent about seriously committing themselves to dancing. Sarah had studied at the University of California at Santa Cruz in the late seventies, and was planning to be a dance major. When she was twenty, she decided to concentrate on dancing, thinking, "OK, this is it, I've got to get my act together and really do well in the dance department." She was told by the department, "You're not serious. You're not committed. We don't want you in the dance department anymore." At the time, she didn't know to say, "Wait a minute. Give me another chance." She said, "OK," and left.

SARAH: When my sister died, I wanted to throw myself into dancing again, for me and for her, and see what I could do with it. Since dancing is normally a nocturnal activity, particularly if you're performing, I was not able to train in aikido because of the schedule conflict. I did that for three years. It became clear that it wasn't going to pan out. There was a constant conflict between money and artistic expression that was not being resolved.

By "conflict" I mean that I didn't apply the most intelligent long-term strategy to being a dancer. I thought, "I want to be performing now." Having taken that approach, I got in situations where I couldn't dance the way I wanted to. So I thought it was time to find something more long-term. Something that's more in tune with the real world, so I could make enough money to support my daughter, but not be so frustrated that I'd come home and start throwing things.

Sarah went back to school and stopped training. She didn't have time to dance or train anymore; she just studied. After she'd been in school a couple of years, she returned to the University of California at Santa Cruz and got her degree in math. She and her husband separated the spring before she started at Santa Cruz. She went on to graduate school where she is now working toward her doctorate in linguistics.

ANDREA: Are there things that you've learned from aikido that you've been able to apply to your life?

SARAH: I seem to generate a lot of conflict. My daughter and I fight all the time. The people I care about, I tend to get into arguments with. The way I handle this is influenced by aikido philosophy: as soon as you can, try to get away from personal attacks on each other and focus on the problem. Don't take things personally.

Both of us have tempers and get mad. I drop that as fast as I can, and try to circle into another arena. I'm fairly good at this.

I've also learned to be aware of the space behind me. I've opened that up, too. When I'm walking, I can feel behind me. I also feel in front of me.

ANDREA: Do you feel safe in the world?

SARAH: I do and I don't. I don't feel threatened by other people very much. I'm not afraid of walking down dark streets by myself. I don't particularly like it, but I know that if anybody messes with me, they're either going to kill me, or they're going to get hurt. No one is ever going to attack me because they think I'm an easy victim. I know that for a fact. If they come at me, they'll find out fast.

On the other hand, you never know what's going to happen. You could be walking down the street and there could be an earthquake, and you could fall into the ground and die. So many freak things can happen. You're always facing death. You just don't think about it. People focus on it when they're walking down the street by themselves, or if they see somebody at the end of an alley. But hazards aren't confined to that. I feel that some women are timid and tend to make it look like they would be easy victims, and perhaps unknowingly they're making themselves targets. I don't think I'm going to do that, ever.

If I'm more effective at self-defense, it's because I have a mean streak in me. If I get mad at somebody, I'm not going to be patient. Even if I am afraid, I won't back down. It's stupid, but I know I've got this temper, and I know I can lose it. If I lost my temper with someone attacking me, it would be scary. That stands me in good stead more than thinking that I will necessarily blend with their energies. Alas. Unfortunately.

ANDREA: You said early on that you weren't strong in following your feelings. Has that changed?

SARAH: I'm in a situation now where my life is how I want it to be. I don't spend as much time letting things put pressure on me. I pretty much structure my life the way I want it.

ANDREA: What do you think your work is here in a larger sense?

SARAH: A lot of people who get involved in aikido think the world should be doing aikido. Everyone should train every day for four hours. They do five hundred wooden sword cuts, and think they're going to get where O'Sensei was, but I think they're fooling themselves. O'Sensei, the founder of aikido, did not become O'Sensei by doing aikido. Aikido came out of O'Sensei after he was already O'Sensei. Think about it. He said, "Aikido is to bring everyone to their true path in life." I don't think that means that everyone should be in a *dojo* all day.

What I'm doing now is close to my true path in life. I'm a very intellectual person, and, as a graduate student and teacher, I'm using my mind in a way that's meaningful. At the same time, I'm in a position to be able to make a contribution. Teaching is a giving profession, and I am in a position to give to people. That means a lot to me, too. I'm not training anymore, but if I view myself as a person going through her path in life, I think I'm getting closer and closer to being and doing what it's right for me to be doing. However it was that I was created, how I was meant to function, I'm getting closer to that, not farther from it. My experience in aikido was valuable. I value it a lot.

ANDREA: What are the signs of a good teacher?

SARAH: When Jack Wada's students get to the black belt level, they look like themselves. They don't look like mini-Jacks. They have their own ideas and their own philosophies. He allows people to grow into themselves.

ANDREA: How does this work?

SARAH: He is very accepting of people as they are. I look at someone and think, "You shouldn't do that. That's terrible. How can you be like that? This is awful."

He thinks, "That's just that person. Oh, he's just like that." He'll spend a lot of time talking to people and hanging out with them, but he doesn't try to change people. That's probably the quality that gives people freedom to find themselves with him. It's a good quality; I admire it.

One of the things I learned from being married to him for so long is to look at people and try and find what about them is good instead of thinking, "That's a bad person. I don't want to be around him."

ANDREA: What doesn't work in teaching aikido?

SARAH: Many people are willing to find fault in others without look-ing at themselves and being honest. It's very easy to get into this situation when you're teaching. Robert Nadeau, another Bay Area teacher, used to always say, "The advanced students should work with the less advanced students, but they should not be talking to them. They should show by example." When brown belts are on the mat talking for a half hour, and no one can get any technique done, this is not the right situation.

Also, some people who have made aikido their entire lives are not what I would call particularly enlightened or even well-behaved.

ANDREA: What did you not like about training?

SARAH: I didn't like people who feel they're superior to everyone else just because they train.

I didn't like the feeling that you have to push yourself past your natural limits. People were always talking about making the world a more natural, harmonious place, but you had to go train every day regardless of whether your knee was broken or not.

I didn't like people who trained while injured, then injured them-selves again and expected people to feel sorry for them—when they knew perfectly well they shouldn't have been training at all. It takes strength of character to get away from that compulsion. I've learned that when things are right for me, I have a lot of energy and dedi-cation, but if that energy and dedication aren't there, it probably means something is wrong. It doesn't mean I'm lazy.

ANDREA: How do you know when it's right?

SARAH: When things are right, I want to be doing the things that I need to be doing. When children act up, people tend to think that there may be some fault in the child-raising, and they need to pun-ish the child or adjust their method. If my daughter Jennifer, nor-mally a very pleasant little child, suddenly becomes temperamental and nasty, I used to worry, "Oh, I have to discipline this child." Then, she'd get sick, and I'd think, "Why couldn't I have mellowed out? She was coming down with something, and she was cranky."

To me, these are similar situations. It's important to learn that people are not automatically going to be the worst that they can be. If they're not as good as they can be, probably there's something wrong that needs to be looked for and confronted.

ANDREA: I think that's healthy.

SARAH: It certainly gets me farther than knocking myself on the head, and trying to barrel through things. There's only so long that I can make myself train twice a day if that's not the right thing for me to be doing. The longer I keep it up the longer I will be hurting myself and going against my own flow.

ANDREA: Does the ability to sense this flow come from your aikido training?

SARAH: I wonder. Aikido certainly gives a dynamic vocabulary for talking about those things. But a lot of those concepts are in yoga, in theatre—they're all over the place. Where did I start to use the tools that I use? I don't know because I've done all those things. I was in theatre arts for a long time.

I look at my daughter Jennifer and I think, "She needs those tools." But I don't know what's the right way for her to get them. Aikido's not a good avenue for her because her father does it, and it's not comfortable for her. She has the same kinds of personality clashes with him that I do. He's very gung ho, and says, "Oh, we're going to do this. Oh, we're going to do that."

She responds, "Just back off." When someone's trying to push her, then she puts her brakes down and says, "I want it to come from me. I don't want it to come from you. Just leave me alone. Now, I'm not going to even do it." I know she needs to learn how to channel and focus her energy. Partly it's because she's young, she needs to be able to relax. Sometimes at night she can't sleep.

ANDREA: How old is she?

SARAH: Twelve. She's an amazingly strong-willed child. I raised her to encourage it, but now I don't think I needed to. She's been choosing her own clothes since she was little. She stands up for herself very well. When I'm behaving in a way that almost anyone else would find overwhelming or overbearing, she'll fight back.

My daughter means a lot to me. I feel fortunate. I look back at my life and think, "All the hard times were worth it because they brought me here, and this is a good place. Or a better place."

ANDREA: How would you describe the internal lessons of martial arts to someone who doesn't know about them?

SARAH: Someone who's good at any martial art will tell you that the goal of martial arts is to find the level of energy where martial arts are no longer necessary. But most martial arts get to that place in such a violent way. There's a strong dichotomy between the professed goal and the actual stuff that they're doing to get there; whereas, in aikido, they go hand in glove. I move in a harmonious way to get to a harmonious place. The movements themselves express that philosophy.

ANDREA: Did the process of doing aikido give you that peace?

SARAH: In some ways, I'm very peaceful; in some ways, I'm not at all. When I was training, I felt that something about having my body go through those blending, smoothing movements was blending and smoothing inside of me. I was becoming less abrasive. I'm not even sure it's true. There are plenty of people who find me plenty abrasive, but they didn't know me when I was eighteen.

ANDREA: What would you say to someone who wanted to start doing aikido?

SARAH: I'd be interested in what they were looking for, and what they expected. I'm concerned when people undertake anything: "What do you think is going to happen? What do you think you're going to be like when you do that?" I don't like to see people get hurt. If they think the whole world's going to change, and all of a sudden turn golden, I say, "Well, I don't think that's going to happen. You probably should be prepared to deal with some disappointment."

But aikido's a good thing to do. It feels good. The people whom I admired in aikido had happy, normal lives and trained because they liked it. One particular guy in San Jose is really successful and he's a nice person. He radiates contentment. He's at the *dojo* maybe once or twice a week. When I was in my gung-ho I've-got-to-train-every-day phase, I was down on him. Now I think, "Look what he did. For years he's been there the same nights every week. He's consistent in a way that people who were fanatic haven't been. He's contributed to the *dojo* by his presence. He did that not out of any desire for self-improvement, but because he likes it. He's not asking aikido to give him anything." I admire that.

Peggy Berger

PEGGY BERGER *grew up in New York. Her main aikido teachers were Robert Nadeau and her husband, Paul Linden. She lives in Columbus, Ohio, with her husband and son. In addition to being a second degree black belt in aikido, Peggy holds a master's degree in Dance Movement Therapy and Counseling. She is an authorized instructor of the Feldenkrais Method and a certified Laban Movement Analyst. She and her husband co-founded the Columbus Center for Movement Studies in Columbus, Ohio, where she teaches classes and does individual work with people seeking to integrate power and love, mind and body, inner child and adult.*

ANDREA: When did you start doing martial arts?

PEGGY: I started in 1978 in California. I was in the master's program at California State University Hayward and was closed out of a dance class. So I took an aikido class instead. Paul Linden was the instructor for the course, but Sue Ann McKean taught the first class. I hadn't done anything really physical before. But seeing Sue Ann, for some reason, I had absolutely no hesitation. It was amazing. I thought, "I want to do that. I absolutely have to do that."

ANDREA: What did you see?

PEGGY: When I refer to this kind of "seeing," what I'm talking about is a kinesthetic sensing—I don't see colors or shapes, but I can sense energies and their qualities. Intuitively, I could see the energy. I could see my limitations, and knew that I could do aikido in spite of them. There was something bigger there than the limits of the personality or the physical body. The physical body wasn't doing the

161

exercise. Rather, something a few feet beyond the physical body just filled up. Suddenly, I could feel it, and a door opened inside of me.

I continued doing aikido because I was interested in developing this other sense I knew was latent in me. I literally did aikido every minute of my life for the first two or three years of training. By that I mean I was constantly trying to tap into a larger self and to understand things from a different perspective. At the time, I was employed by the Social Security Administration in Oakland, California. There was a lot of conflict in the office. I would spend a great deal of time centering myself in order to work with what was happening in the office and with the manager. I was always coming back and trying to settle into my own center.

I'd go to aikido classes to learn more about energy and centering. Very often, just being in class provided an energy state that I'd "drink up," to change myself. Then I'd go back out into my life, and somehow I was the same old person because I hadn't learned how to make the transition between the mat and my life. I didn't know how to keep the energy going in myself or how to notice when it stopped flowing and then be able to tap it again. After being around it for quite a while, I discovered how to feel my own way to get there. One thing that helped me learn to apply it was that my aikido buddies and I would continuously talk about it, think about it, and struggle with how to use it.

At the time the whole world of Eastern thought was opening up for me. I thought, "Some guru taps you on the head, your chakras open up, and that's it." When I started training, a door had opened, and I was in this room with this gorgeous stuff. After I trained a while, the honeymoon ended, and then I had to do the work.

ANDREA: The work?

PEGGY: Work on myself. When Paul moved to Columbus shortly after I started aikido, I continued training with his instructor, Robert Nadeau. When I studied with Nadeau, I went into the *dojo,* and the work was happening. I just let it come into me. After I left California, I had to do the work myself because the other aikido teachers and students I encountered were doing different things in their

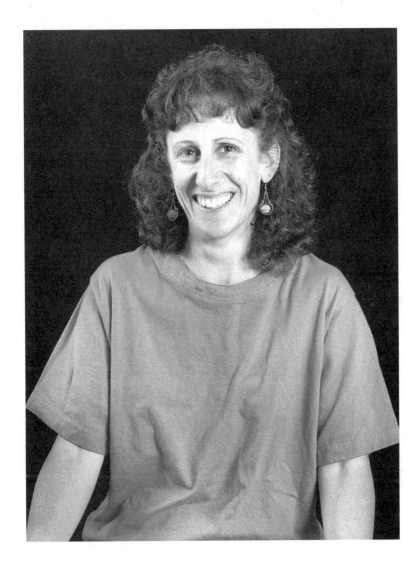

practice. I felt alone with my inner work. But I knew that if I did aikido with that special experience internally, then I got something very valuable.

ANDREA: When you loved training, what did you love about it?

PEGGY: I felt whole, alive, energized. I liked myself. And I liked other people better.

After three years in California, Peggy moved to New York in 1979 to train in Laban Movement Analysis, a movement discipline which she had been studying before she began aikido. In Laban training, she learned to observe closely the expressive elements and dynamic range of movement.

PEGGY: I trained at two different *dojos*. They both had very good aikido, but they were not doing the aikido that I knew. I was not very good physically at aikido when I left California. But energetically, I was skilled and had this idea that aikido was about energetic, not physical development. I thought aikido was about changing consciousness and getting out of the personality. I never understood it as a martial art, or understood the relationship between *budo* and growth. After I left California, it took me four years to begin to understand that one way of practicing isn't right and another way isn't wrong, but that there are different roads to understanding what aikido has to offer and that different people need to learn in different ways.

ANDREA: Did you eventually learn the physical aspect of the moves, and was it valuable for you to do so?

PEGGY: I fought it tooth and nail, yet learning the techniques was absolutely invaluable for me. I needed aikido to get into my body, to get here on the earth plane. I learned that the body provides the feedback about what's going on in other levels of the self. It also concretizes the coping strategies that have been used for survival. We all cope with life in various ways. Often, old, habitual coping strategies have a lot of pain and negativity attached to them. Our coping strategies shape how we move our bodies and how we hold our bodies. By gently, closely observing and using that embodied information, we can understand what our life choices have been and begin to make other, better choices.

While Peggy was pursuing certification in Laban Movement Analysis, she began studying the Feldenkrais method to become a Feldenkrais instructor. Paul came out from Ohio to visit her during the Feldenkrais training, and they moved back to Ohio together in 1980. Peggy started teaching aikido when she was a 4th kyu because there were only two black belts at the Ohio State University aikido club and if they weren't available to teach, she, as the next highest in rank, had to teach.

ANDREA: What are your feelings about rank and testing?

PEGGY: What is most valuable to me is direct, specific feedback about who I am and what I'm doing, so rank as such is secondary for me. However, rank is an acknowledgment of the inner and outer work a student has done.

ANDREA: Did you want the black belt?

PEGGY: I wanted the black belt so that I could teach with a little bit of authority, without getting crap from guys. And also so that women would appreciate that there was somebody here who had a black belt. I wanted my *nidan* because I wanted to be acknowledged for the hard work I had done both emotionally and physically.

In terms of the rank and the hierarchy in aikido, in some ways I understand more than a fifth, sixth, or seventh *dan*. Yet, in some ways, I can't even see as much as a fifth *kyu* can see. A lot of people in aikido believe in a hierarchical form of relationship between more advanced and less advanced aikidoists. They believe knowledge flows only one way, from the top down. I don't believe that. I believe everybody has a human awareness and sensitivity that deserves respect. I can learn from the beginner maybe even more than I do from an advanced person. Beginners show me my openings, where I'm patient or not patient. They push my buttons a whole lot more, and I'm challenged. And even a beginner can see things about my aikido technique that I may have missed.

ANDREA: But don't teachers know more about power?

PEGGY: Power is important. In the martial arts, you're working on developing power. However, if you don't develop compassion and respect with power, you just abuse it. The work Paul and I do is about balancing power with compassion. Without that, power is exercised irresponsibly.

ANDREA: How can one develop compassion?

PEGGY: Traditional aikido training deals a lot with *hara,* the center which is located in the belly. It doesn't teach about softening the chest, which is the source of heart energy, and letting the heart connect down to the *hara,* which then connects down to the floor. It is true that you can't open your chest or your heart until you can support it on a good *hara* foundation. However, when you let your belly go *and* you soften your chest, you get a lot more power than you get if your chest is tight. But, it's a very different quality from what most people think of as power. I use the term "integrity" for this state of being. Not only is heart integrated with power, but we have the psychological integrity to assert our own being-ness in the world.

At this point, Peggy stood up to demonstrate. She placed her feet in hanmi, *a position over which her body could stand easily and comfortably. She looked rooted to the ground. Her knees were slightly bent, not locked. Her belly was relaxed and her shoulders were down. With one hand she drew an invisible line from her heart, through her belly to the floor.*

PEGGY: This is physical. I can feel the connection going through my belly, down through my feet to the middle of the earth. I sense my whole body softening, including my pelvic floor muscles, my vagina, and my anal sphincter muscles. Everything has settled down, strongly and solidly, connected to the earth. Once I can let my feet support me, then I can afford to open my heart. That also applies to relationships. If you can't maintain your own boundaries, your own power base, your own integrity, you can't afford to love. If I'm tight in my heart, clenching my jaw, or my arms are rigid with overextension, I may be able to stand on my own two feet, but on some level I don't trust that I can safely reach out to connect with somebody else. There's a distancing. It's like a steel edge. But when my chest softens, suddenly the edge is gone. I feel like I'm on a cloud, but a strongly grounded cloud. It's soft, deep, and extensive, and whoever I'm with is just part of that cloud. When my muscles are tight, the cloud that encompasses both me and those near me, friends or attackers alike, vanishes. There's a barrier. I can see it and feel it. It affects the way I relate. On the aikido mat, when I've been thrown by a person who is fully open, I feel like I've been taken care of. I don't get hurt. *Ukemi* is easy. However, when I'm thrown by somebody who is open in their belly, but holds their neck tightly, clenches their jaw, or constricts their chest muscles, I feel their power, but there's no cushioning. In this situation, I don't feel connected to them, and my *ukemi* is more hesitant; my falls often hurt.

I remember a time when Nadeau threw me. He didn't hold back on his power. He was able to do what he needed to do, and I felt totally protected. It felt as if I were floating on that cloud. Even when I landed on this hard mat. At the time, I had only been practicing a year or so and I did not yet know how to do hard falls, but I was protected.

ANDREA: What changed in you as you began to practice this kind of awareness?

PEGGY: I began to feel the fears that I used to numb myself to. Previously, I hadn't experienced much of my own fear because I didn't have the security to trust that I could get through it. This often comes up for people in our *dojo*. As they grow stronger, and become more capable of centering and settling, sometimes they feel worse, because they can afford to let deeply buried feelings of pain come through now.

ANDREA: How do you foster a healthy student/teacher relationship?

PEGGY: Good teachers don't allow students to become dependent on them. I put a great deal of energy into giving my students the tools to grow and work and explore on their own. This way they don't need me to fix them. I don't socialize a whole lot with my students, which is hard for me because I like them a lot. But there needs to be a certain distance. If I relate to them as *sensei* and simultaneously relate to them personally, there is a confusion between my roles as an impartial guide in their growth and as a person with needs.

On another level, I recognize that, unlike some of my teachers, I don't have the ability to simply *put* somebody in an energy state. Instead, what I give students, and I think this is very healthy, is the ability to notice what they're doing, and take responsibility for it. They say, "Hey, my *uke* is giving me a bad attack." I'll say, "Well, that might be true. But everybody always wants to blame the *uke*. Let's look at what *you're* doing." I don't look at the execution of the move in only a technical way, but rather I might say, "How do you keep yourself from having a clear mind? What are you doing that makes it difficult for you to move effectively? Why aren't you breathing? Perhaps you don't yet know details of the technique. But breathe. See what happens."

They'll say, "Oh, my God, I feel sick to my stomach when I breathe." or "Oh, I never breathe when I fall down on that side. I only breathe when I go down on the other side." I'll say, "That's great information. Work with it." Or I'll say, "Choose one quality. You might need to relax your shoulders. You might want to pay attention to your breathing. Maybe, concentrate on moving with a feeling of verticality. Choose one thing, and play with it for a month. I'm not going to tell you what's right for you. You choose." Those are obvious ways to help people notice what they're doing. There are more subtle ways.

I don't want glamour. I may distance myself because I think that's appropriate, but I don't try to convey that I'm great. I'm just a human being. So, if somebody does try to kowtow to me or bow to me all the time, I'll say, "You don't need to do that." I do not have people call me *sensei*. I can very quickly tell if somebody is trying to suck my energy. I don't like it, and I don't let it continue. I turn it back real quick.

ANDREA: Why?

PEGGY: I'm sensitive to issues of abuse. It's abusive when somebody uses their power to disempower another. It's abusive when a teacher says, "I have the truth. And you follow my truth, or you go to a different *dojo*." Many teachers fall into the trap of believing that they are something more than just another student on the path. And I also won't let students disempower themselves by giving me their power. I believe that helping students stop or prevent such energy abuse is part of being a good teacher.

ANDREA: What projects are you most involved with now?

PEGGY: I'm working toward a degree and license in clinical counseling. I'm the mother of a six-year-old and I take my job as mother very seriously. I also teach at our movement center. I most enjoy teaching a self-defense class for sexual abuse survivors. It takes weeks before we get to physical self-defense techniques. We do exercises. For instance: you have a person walk toward you and you learn to say, "Stop," when that person comes to the edge of what's comfortable for you. In this way you find out where your boundaries are. If you're not in your body, it takes a long time to get cues about this. We work with centering and empowering. Once we start doing physical self-defense, every time we do a technique, we then process for an hour and a half afterward.

ANDREA: What is hard about the work that you're doing?

PEGGY: It's terrifying. On the professional level, it took ten years to establish the Columbus Center for Movement Studies. Aikido is just one part, an important part, of the whole work we are doing. There is a fundamental process of awareness and empowerment underlying both our aikido and our other movement work. Nobody wanted this kind of stuff. They wanted to go do passive body work, go to a guru, leave their bodies, do channeling, and get a quick fix. They wanted to give away the power.

On a different level, it's hard because when people start becoming present and working on their power, pain comes up about why they weren't present previously. They may not even have a concrete reason why. They can find out after a while. We help people recover lost memories. The only way to heal is to go deep inside to where the pain is, and who wants to go where the pain is? The only way to do better aikido is to open up, and who wants to open up when you're used to being scared and not looking at what is scaring you? Who wants to admit they're scared? Who wants to give up the steel-like power, the armor of numbness, for something that seems like it's not going to work? We've been taught by our past history that this heart power and integrity makes us vulnerable, but that was because when we opened our hearts before, we did so without developing the physical base of support that I talked about earlier.

People don't want to go live where the memories, the pain, and the vulnerability are. And yet it's the only way to develop power. The process which Paul and I are teaching involves trying to push through it anyway.

ANDREA: When you say "push through it," do you mean force?

PEGGY: No. I mean "be there." Have a willingness to stay present with the places inside you where you know you might die. Because if you had been there when you were a kid, you would have died. At least part of you did get put on hold for a long time. "Pushing through it" involves being willing to go there anyway because the adult intellectual part of you knows that now you've developed the tools.

ANDREA: What other things do you do to support this process?

PEGGY: As a teacher, part of my job is to trust my students' present-day adult integrity. When they try to slip away from that, I won't let them, verbally or physically. I do physical self-defense techniques with them a lot. I'll attack them. If they say, "I don't want to be attacked," I'll say, "Too bad. You've got to do it, and you can do it. The only part of you that thinks you can't do it is your mind. Your body can do it. You can do it." After they've done the technique, their pain comes up. They can afford to feel, because they've developed the inner strength to handle it through the physical expression.

Then, we'll have them do something that will kick in the new energy so it's not just the old pattern. Maybe we will role-play the old memory, only this time they'll push away or throw off the person posing as the attacker. Something goes "click" inside them; and after that there might be pain, sadness, grief, and fury, but they're not numb anymore. They're alive.

Choosing to do the work is hard, but the work is so loving. When a person manifests who they really are, either in pain or joy, they are exquisitely beautiful.

ANDREA: Do you feel safe in the world?

PEGGY: No.

ANDREA: Have you ever had to use your aikido in self-defense?

PEGGY: No, I haven't. Once when I was walking in New York City, after I'd been practicing aikido for two or three years, I was walking down a street and this guy jumped off his truck right in front of me. I thought he was jumping on me, and I spontaneously turned to face him. I was totally ready to defend myself. I was shocked I did it. He laughed, and I laughed; and I walked on. That's the closest that I've ever gotten to using it.

I've noticed you haven't asked me about killing.

ANDREA: No. It's never crossed my mind.

PEGGY: It's a martial art. We are talking about all this learning and spirituality, and martial art, *budo,* is about killing. We've talked about the physically based aikido technique as opposed to the energy-based aikido technique, but we haven't mentioned that the physically based technique is important because if you can't kill, you can't heal. It took a long time to convince me that I even cared about killing. And it wasn't until I became a mother that I understood. I would kill if somebody were hurting my kid. I think it's a mammalian response. If somebody is out to get your baby, you do what you need to do, effectively, without anger, hatred, or fear. You just do it. You can even care about the attacker. As a matter of fact, if you don't care, then there's a problem.

ANDREA: How does being able to kill enable you to be able to heal?

PEGGY: If I know how to do a technique subtly enough to damage a joint or break a bone, then I know how to do the reverse of that to help it. Aikido is a very close contact art. You have to feel the subtleties of the intent of your partner, your attacker. If you can feel the intent, then you can work with it, to your partner's advantage or disadvantage.

ANDREA: When does healing transpire?

PEGGY: That takes place more in the hands-on work that I do. If you can feel your client's intent, you can be there with them, with their intent and help them go toward that intent. You can help that intention come to awareness when it's buried, and then make choices about whether that truly is an appropriate intent or not.

On a physical level, this makes people a lot safer. They have a clarity that helps them know how to move comfortably and effectively. On an emotional level, that's true, too. If people know their patterns and the significance of them, then they can begin to discern if the patterns are appropriate present-time responses or old patterns triggered by a present situation. By changing their patterns of intention, people can become more balanced, centered, open, and expansive, and they can make new physical and emotional choices.

ANDREA: What did weapons training in aikido mean to you?

PEGGY: I used to hate the idea of weapons. A couple of years ago, I started liking weapons. They feel like an extension, just the next step. Earlier they had seemed like another appendage, and I didn't even know what to do with the ones I had started with. Weapons have come up a lot now that I have a child, a boy. People say, "Oh, you shouldn't let him play with weapons, or make believe he's shooting guns and stuff." How can I, who can kill with a hand, with a finger, tell my kid that he can't pretend that he's fighting? I don't feel like weapons are any worse than fingers, or words.

In "real life," words and weapons can devastate and kill. Training on the mat is not about hostility or fighting. We're working with integrity, and with power. We're working towards a physical energy state that will allow us to be who we are.

ANDREA: What is the overriding theme of what you do?

PEGGY: The work that we're doing on this planet is to get present. Instead of going outside ourselves toward something bigger than we are, our job is to bring whatever's bigger on this planet through our physical beings. In Ohio, after ten years of work, the middle-

American community is just now opening to what Paul and I and others who do work like ours have to offer.

ANDREA: What do you think you offer them?

PEGGY: The first word that came to me was "hope." Maybe because I'm working with so many incest survivors who have been gone, "out of their bodies" for good reasons. So, for me and for the people I teach, becoming aware of and strong in the body is like coming home, and finding out who we really are. Being a human being doesn't mean what we thought it meant, with all of the limitations. There's more.

ANDREA: What is the more?

PEGGY: The role of the warrior is not to fight and to create separation, but rather to create integrity and identity, and with this, to create connection. If we're here and we keep our hearts open, we will care about our planet. We won't treat our kids like nuisances. We'll care about them. And we'll care about our environment rather than destroy it. We will care about *people,* not businesses or governments or countries, but human beings, like ourselves, who share this planet with us and come in all different colors and sizes and with many different lifestyles and values. We will create this connectedness while maintaining our own individual integrity. First, we must become connected to ourselves as individuals, then to our families, then the community, the nation, the planet, and whatever's beyond that.

Cheryl Reinhardt

CHERYL REINHARDT *was born and raised in the New York metro-politan area. Her main aikido teacher was Robert Nadeau. She currently lives and works in Oakland, California. Cheryl is known for her expertise as a Feldenkrais Practitioner, aikidoist, and teacher. People recommended Cheryl to me three years ago when I was having back problems. Two people who didn't know each other urged me to see her to help heal my back. I did, and it did help. She invited me to take her aikido class, which I immediately loved.*

Cheryl was a student in the first North American Feldenkrais Professional Training Program. Moshe Feldenkrais—the Israeli physicist and judo expert who created Functional Integration® and Awareness Through Movement®—began training practitioners in a system of two original ways of learning through movement based on the working of the nervous system.

Cheryl's office, where the interview took place, is a warm wood-panelled room. One wall is mostly windows, providing a view of tall trees and lots of greenery. Despite the fact that I know we are in the city, sitting on her work table and speaking with her, I feel as if I am in a posh tree house in the middle of a forest. The office contains bookshelves filled with books and photos, a handmade wooden file cabinet, the "table" on which clients lie as she works, heat lamps, a chair and a desk. Cheryl sits in the dark wooden arm-chair, the back of which is elaborately carved with the face of a wise and merry man. To my left, on a stand, hangs a human skeleton of a woman who was about five feet tall while alive.

ANDREA: How did you start doing aikido?

CHERYL: I began studying aikido because I sensed such a disparity between what I was doing when I worked with clients and what I experienced Moshe doing as he set to work. Moshe had such a tremendous presence about him. It became apparent to me that his years of judo were one of the contributing factors to his power to heal.

At this same time, a friend of mine who was studying aikido by night, studied with Moshe by day. I had the good fortune to learn the philosophy of aikido over lunch each day. Learning the philosophy is a bit different than stepping on the mat. It took me quite a few years to join the training at the *dojo*.

ANDREA: What was it like for you to start aikido?

CHERYL: It was great. I stepped on the mat and I loved it. I loved moving. I loved moving with a partner. I loved the philosophy. Early in my training, my teacher turned to me and said, "When you're a black belt..." How did he know I was going to stay long enough? Well, he knew and I knew that I was there for the long haul. I knew I was home. I stepped on the mat, and it felt then the way it still feels now. It feels juicy and exciting. It was a real place to learn.

ANDREA: Explain what you mean by this experience of feeling "juicy."

CHERYL: "Juicy" is a reminder of what is truly human—a sense of a connection to yourself and other human beings... the ability to sense truly who someone else is and how they move. This is part of the magic of training in aikido. The aikido mat was not the first place I experienced this sensation. But my recognition of the mat as a place where aliveness is the norm brought about my commitment to aikido. To blend with a partner, to throw and be thrown really does move your blood in an exciting way. It opens the door to your inner life, your depth. Some people access this through their art, or their writing, or their music. Jazz musicians experience a similar phenomenon when they jam together.

ANDREA: What is "depth" in terms of an inner life?

CHERYL: When I speak of depth, I'm referring to access to an inner life: being close enough to yourself that you live the life you want to be living, making decisions from choice rather than habit or convention. You can travel the path to your depth through movement. For example, begin sensing where your attention is. This is the starting point. Often people's minds are fraught with tedious details. The smallest of movements brings the attention into the body. You start to sense your own breathing, and your ribs moving as you breathe. You might sense your skin, the weight of your hips sitting on the chair, and your feet in contact with the ground. Soon there is a sense of roundness, like having hula hoops of aliveness all around yourself. This is sensed down through your hips, through your knees, and then, down to your feet. It's almost like these hula hoops get bigger and bigger. You experience a sense of depth beneath and around yourself.

ANDREA: How do you keep your power as a student?

CHERYL: When I began aikido at the Turk Street *dojo,* before San Francisco's Opera Plaza existed and the highlight of the area was the Doggie Diner, there was confusion about how to empower people. In the martial arts, students are learning about an internal power as well as physical power.

After training almost daily for three-and-a-half years, I was off the mat for a month. Having been away for what seemed like a tremendously long time, I watched class with virgin eyes. I said to my teacher, Robert Nadeau (it was a beautiful moment), "Bob, I got it. We really need to learn how to be ourselves on the mat, not Bob Nadeau. We need to learn to have the power in our own systems, and not be imitating you." He used that in his teaching from then on, because it was important. People struggle so much against "the power thing." That's why it was so helpful to both of us. It felt so simple. I saw that what really worked was for us to somehow find our own individuality on the mat. It is difficult when you're learning because you need models, and you need guidance. But then you individuate.

ANDREA: For many people I've talked with, taking one's own power has been a real turning point.

CHERYL: That's what our generation of women aikidoists achieved. My teaching is specifically geared to empower my students.

ANDREA: What was so compelling about aikido?

CHERYL: It was just the place I went to breathe and to gain perspective. It was my church, my temple.

ANDREA: Is there anything you want to say about that time around training for your black belt?

CHERYL: We're talking about *shodan,* the black belt test. The person who put in a lot of time with me was a cop from Menlo Park. He was consistent in his training with me. I was able to work with him without being on the emotional roller coaster which I had often experienced in training prior to that point. We kept training, and training. My grasp and understanding of aikido broadened. I felt safer in my body. My body became a true friend that I could depend on. I learned a sense of well-being.

The test was a marvelous experience. I was out there beforehand getting ready, and another friend said to me, "Just sit down, Cheryl. Don't burn it all out right now." He was right. So I just sat down. My challenge in that test was to stay connected to my *uke* (the person who was attacking) during the whole test. It felt beautiful and powerful. Time seemed to slow down. My mouth was very dry. My *uke,* the judges, the room and the attacks I was asked to respond to all seemed to take on a special clarity.

I'm 5 feet 2 inches. In my multiple attack, all the guys coming in were over a foot taller. It was a wonderful and joyous event.

ANDREA: What do you mean by "stay connected"?

CHERYL: It's like dancing with a partner. Moshe Feldenkrais often said his work was analogous to dancing: "The way to work with people is to dance with them. If you really want to learn to dance, you find a person who knows how to dance very well, and fall in love with them. And you very quickly learn to dance." Good aikido is a beautiful and fulfilling dance.

As Cheryl talked about the dance her hands were moving toward me and toward her, alternating in a flowing motion.

ANDREA: I heard you took your second degree black belt test when you were quite pregnant.

CHERYL: Actually, it has been my experience that as soon as I was pregnant, I was really pregnant. I was in my first trimester and I didn't feel very good. Maybe that's why my son is the way he is—he started life amidst a *nidan* test.

I continued teaching aikido right through my ninth month. Then I started teaching again a month after the birth. My kids have both been around my teaching on the mat a lot. They've been to class many times. I have a mat in the downstairs of my home that they play on. They are at home with the mat, and with what goes on on the mat. There is a feeling in the *dojo* that isn't experienced in a lot of places. It's a special place for a kid to absorb information about living.

ANDREA: Did you want a black belt? Did you sense that other people wanted rank?

CHERYL: I did not begin aikido planning to become a black belt. I did not go in planning to become a martial artist or to gain rank. As I think about what I do now, I know that one of my real strengths in teaching is that I teach martial arts to people who have no self-image of being martial artists. No part of me could imagine myself a martial artist. In that vein, a black belt was not something I even considered attaining.

I worked harder for that black belt than I'd ever worked for anything in my life. Scholastic achievements had been relatively easy. Aikido wasn't like that for me. I couldn't be lazy. I was small. I had to really train.

I trained a lot. I put in an awful lot of time, and many changes occurred in me, in the process of training for a black belt. I had to learn how to work with the energy raging through my body. Only after becoming a black belt did my true aikido begin. I was faced with the challenge of learning how to integrate being a black belt with my life.

To get through that training—I hate to discourage anyone—took me years. I'm hoping and praying my students will get it much faster. But I am seeing that aikido is a slow long study.

Applying harmony, blending, universal love to daily life is very, very challenging. And I don't think that aikido, in and of itself, is magic. Just becoming a black belt doesn't change one's way of living. I feel truly challenged to integrate having become a black belt into all the situations I deal with, in my work, my family, and myself.

ANDREA: How have you applied it recently?

CHERYL: My own inner work is just that! To live impeccably, as a twentieth-century woman warrior—I am applying what I've been trained to do at every step.

ANDREA: Can you say more about taking care of yourself?

CHERYL: Taking care of myself is an essential aspect of what we're speaking of here. I work with people individually, day in and day out. I do an alternative to many forms of therapy. I see my work as helping people get as close to their essential selves as possible.

I didn't take care of myself on the aikido mat. We got thrown around. There's a macho-ness. I'd get on that mat, and, especially in my earlier training days, just keep going and going. I broke a bone in a couple of places and I kept going. I went back to training too soon after I broke that bone. I wasn't taking care of myself. But aikido came first. There was something so important to learn that it came before taking care of myself. I don't regret it for one minute, but I wouldn't do it the same way now.

We must take care of ourselves: get enough food, enough sleep. It sounds so mundane, but it's the basics. I teach this to people. Smart people—professionals, doctors—don't know how to take care of themselves. People are trained to put other people first, and put their work first. They don't know to get enough sleep. They don't know to eat. People are tremendously resistant to being helped with taking the time to do things that feed their system. There was a recent study which proved what we've known for awhile: it's a physiological reality that your emotions are connected to your body. People have a hard time being kind to themselves. I had to train myself to be kind, to be good to myself and others.

ANDREA: Did learning how to take care of yourself come out of the Feldenkrais work?

CHERYL: No. The Feldenkrais work was as brutal as the aikido training in a different way. Moshe was a hard teacher. He was marvelous, a genius but he didn't always make us feel good about ourselves. It came after training with Moshe Feldenkrais, and after my aikido training. After working with hundreds of people, who I kept seeing didn't know how to take care of themselves, I figured that maybe I had better take care of *myself*. And that's taken a lot of energy and guts because there's not a lot of support for it. I have had a teacher who has guided me in the integration of my work and taking care of myself. Her name is Kathleen Riordan Speeth, herself a writer, teacher, and psychologist.

ANDREA: What you're talking about is not narcissism. It's something else.

CHERYL: Being in good health isn't narcissism. Because if you're in good health, you have much more ability to see others, to hear others, to take care of others if it's necessary, and to teach others.

ANDREA: What kinds of physical things had you done before aikido?

CHERYL: I was not an athlete. I danced. I did yoga, I taught yoga. I performed. The Feldenkrais work is all about using the body, so I had learned and practiced a lot of body discipline. But, I learned to be *in* my body in aikido. I performed after I started aikido, and those were the first performances that felt like true performances. I learned from aikido what dance performance is: the qualities of using myself and extending energy. I'm sure some dance students and drama students learned that in class, but I learned it in aikido. I had a very dramatic teacher.

ANDREA: Can you talk about the work you do and how you integrate your life and your work?

CHERYL: I have a private practice and I teach group classes. When I work with someone, I am doing hands-on Feldenkrais work. This is usually gentle guided movements. I'm listening to the functioning of the individual and feeding it back to them, via touch. The hope is to re-educate a person's habitual way of thinking as well as their physical holding patterns. I listen to people, reading their tone of voice, the way they are holding their body, where their eyes look as they speak. I work to provide them with a more focused reflection of themselves. I have learned that learning only occurs when the student feels safe. It is then that they can tap their own potential. The result is self-empowerment. The problems that people come to me with, are then not so overwhelming when they feel safe and centered.

I work with each person differently, in my individual practice, as well as in class. I thoroughly enjoy interacting with each individual.

I recently had a very gratifying session with a woman I've worked with for many years. Grace has a large family, many of whom I've met and worked with over the years. On this particular day, Grace arrived late and was talking before we could get into my office. She sat down on my Feldenkrais table and was telling me four stories at once. My job seemed to be to help her sort through what was essential to her. Her cousins were staying at her house and the dynamics between them were mostly wonderful. At the same time, she was concerned about an old family dynamic that was rearing its head. She was also worried about her mother's impending visit and the effect it might have on her husband and daughter. Grace reported this to me amidst all the trivial details that were on her mind, both related and unrelated.

I listened carefully. I was breathing evenly, continually aware of my back against my chair, and my feet on the floor as we spoke. We did some table work. I was listening with my hands as well as my other senses. She calmed down and remembered her inner life. As she remembered herself as a musician as well as a family member, she could see her way through the web of confusion. She was able to feel how much she loves these members of her family, and that this was more important than everyone else's agenda. As she felt her truer self, she felt freed of her old role in the family drama.

Grace came back one week later, glowing. She was quite proud of her success. She had been situated in a typical familial web. Her accomplishment was maintaining her sense of center and well-being, while still loving her family.

ANDREA: My experience of your work is that it is magical. Probably from your perspective there's something more ordinary about it?

CHERYL: Yes and no. It's the magic that affects me. I know I've done well when I feel the magic. But, I am practical. I draw from my common sense a great deal. But I also draw from the magic of the connection, of being able to blend.

ANDREA: What scares you about the present moment? How do you integrate it into the process of living?

CHERYL: What is most frightening is what's out of control—will the environment be destroyed? Will there be a nuclear holocaust? What will we do in the event of a major earthquake? Aside from those events, fear is not the issue. I do feel truly challenged to keep remembering to use all of what I know, with different individuals, in different circumstances.

ANDREA: How do you find the appropriate response?

CHERYL: Mostly I give myself enough time. I don't respond at the moment. Often I either sit down or lie down and just let it run around in my mind. I breathe and feel my bones, forgetting about it and remembering that I really am much bigger than my little problems. Feeling that 360° connectedness, what's in front of me and in back of me, the room, the earth, the sky, the whole bigness, will often give me the perspective to respond the way I want to.

ANDREA: A lot of women haven't been able to integrate the process of doing what they love to do and making a living. Can you talk about how you came to that?

CHERYL: I did it patiently. I started out having a good setup. I taught school part time. I was young, so I didn't have to bring in a whole lot of money to earn a living. And I didn't have expectations that I could be doing it all immediately. It just seemed like the only way to go: put one foot in front of the other, and pray that people would call me. And one person called, and then two people called, then three people, then eight.

ANDREA: Is there anything you would say to coach people who want to move toward what's essential in them?

CHERYL: There are many paths back to our essential self. Movement, art, music, writing, to name a few. Choose one or two or let them choose you. Then practice *every day.* Let your inner life come before the trivial in your life: your lists, your magazines, and your catalogues can wait. If movement works for you, do a small quiet moving meditation *every single day.* Set a timer so you can get lost in your work. You'll know what form is right for you because you'll delight in it. Your breathing will become fuller. Your days will feel more fulfilled. Your inner life will be awakened. This is truly moving from your center.

ANDREA: How is the Cheryl of today different from the Cheryl who first stepped on that mat?

CHERYL: I'm an adult, accountable for my actions.

Glossary

Aikido: *Ai* means harmony, *ki* means spirit, *do* means way or path. Hence, the way of harmony. Aikido is a Japanese martial art developed in the twentieth century by Morihei Ueshiba, who died in 1969. One interviewee said, "Aikido is an inner growth process that happens to take a physical form. For me, aikido provides a structure, a language, specific guidelines, and some rules. For some people, it's strictly physical, a superb form of self-defense."

Belts: In America, rank is often conferred after testing one's ability to handle certain attacks well. The number of responses one is required to know increases with each test. Sometimes rank is given in the absence of testing.

Black belt is considered the highest skill level. There are different levels of black belt, *shodan* (first), *nidan* (second), etc. (see below).

In Japan, one wears a white belt until one gets a black belt. In America, often one first wears a white belt, then blue, then brown, then black.

Ranking levels from beginner to most advanced:

Kyu: (pronounced like "Q") There are five *kyu* levels to pass through before taking the black belt test. A beginner comes on the mat as a sixth *kyu*.

White Belt: fifth and sixth *kyu*. In *dojos* in America where a colored belt system is used, a beginner wears a white belt.

Blue Belt: third and fourth *kyu*. In some *dojos*, a white belt is worn until black belt level.

186 / WOMEN IN AIKIDO

Nikkyu: second *kyu*. Also called first degree brown belt. Two exams away from black belt.

Ikkyu: second degree brown belt (the rank before black belt). Also called "first *kyu*."

Brown Belt: first and second *kyu*.

Shodan: first degree black belt

Nidan: second degree black belt

Sondan: third degree black belt

Yondan: fourth degree black belt

Godan: fifth degree black belt

Black Belt: A level rank or skill in a martial art. For Americans, this term may imply a level of mastery.

Blend: To blend is to combine your energy with your partner's so that you feel the combination. Your energies feel unified in one flow, yet you fully sense your own muscular organization and balance, and your breathing. "Blending is sensing the direction and intensity of the attack and turning to move with it or redirect it," one interviewee said.

Body Work: A general term for physical therapy. Examples of forms of body work include such hands-on disciplines as massage, Feldenkrais, Alexander technique, Rolfing, acupressure, Reichian work, etc.

Bokken: Short wooden practice sword.

Budo or Bujitsu: The martial way or the path of the martial artist which encompasses a spiritual perspective.

Dan: Black belt level. (*Shodan* is first degree black belt, *nidan* is second degree, etc.) See **Belts.**

Dojo: A martial arts training hall, place where one studies.

186

Falling: Aikido training teaches students how to fall down safely using rolling and "high falls." Usually a successful attack concludes with the attacker having "fallen." One interviewee said, "There's something wonderful about reclaiming falling on the ground as an experience that's delightful and energizing. We all touched this when we were kids."

Gi: Training uniform: usually a white cotton top which ties closed, and drawstring trousers.

Hakama: *Samurai* skirt. Black or blue split skirt worn over the *gi* trousers by male black belts, and by women whenever they feel like it.

Hanmi: Half-open stance where one's weight feels evenly balanced on both feet. The knees are slightly bent with one foot about a foot in front of the other.

Hara: Called the "center" of the body, located approximately three inches below the navel. The "seat" of the life energy or *ki*.

Hombu Dojo: Aikido international headquarters and training hall in Hombu, Japan.

Irimi: Entering directly into an attack.

Iwama: Japanese city where Morihei Ueshiba, the founder of aikido, had his country home and a *dojo*.

Jo: A five-foot-long wooden staff used as a weapon in the martial arts.

Kata: A prearranged exercise used as a learning technique.

Ki: The subtle and maneuverable life-giving energy that flows through all of us. Similar to Chinese *Chi* or the Hindu *Prana*.

One interviewee said, "I couldn't define it. It's an experience. But I can describe feelings I've had to do with *ki*. It can feel warm or cold. It can feel like a wave. It can feel hard or soft. The images that come to mind are water or air, sometimes electricity, or fire. There's a sense of a moving through. I don't know where it comes from. Sometimes I feel I'm simply a channel, a physical something that this *ki* shines, flows, or exudes through." A bit like a flower that draws up and exudes water, or receives in light and changes it into form.

Ki-ai-ing: Letting forth a burst of sound that comes naturally from deep within the belly. The sound often is quite loud, abrupt, and strange. An outflowing of *ki* energy through the voice.

Kiatsu: A laying on of hands to sense physical energy deeply, through the tissue, bones, and musculature. Moving or allowing energy to flow in a way that is healing to that part that is injured.

Ki Flow Practices: Warm-up exercises.

Kyu: There are five *kyu* levels to pass through before taking the black belt test. A beginner comes on the mat as a sixth *kyu*. See **Belts.**

Ma-ai: "Harmony of space" or correct distance between the attacker and the person who receives the attack, as in "I feel most comfortable with this much distance between us. This creates the most stable situation."

The Mat: The padding on the floor in a *dojo* where training takes place. The traditional mat is made of *tatami,* a kind of straw. They're harder than the mats generally used in the United States, which are often gymnastic mats.

Morihei: Abundant peace. The first name of the founder of aikido.

Nage: One who receives an "attack," and implements the technique.

Nikkyo: An aikido technique in which, as one interviewee put it, "the wrist is bent, in such a way that the person really can only go down on their knees. Otherwise, he or she will encounter severe pain."

O'Sensei: Great teacher. The name that Morihei Ueshiba, the founder of aikido, was called.

Pinning: Completing an attack, so the attacker cannot move. Also referred to as "the pin." Released by the attacker tapping the mat with the unpinned hand, or body part, to signify "enough."

Randori: Multiple attack practice. An attack on one person by several others. A standard part of the first degree black belt exam.

Seiza: A formal sitting position on one's knees, with one's spine fairly straight. The classic martial arts sitting posture.

Sensei: A polite way of referring to a teacher in a *dojo*. Each *dojo* has its own etiquette about who is referred to as *sensei*.

Shodan: First degree black belt. See **Belts**.

Shomen: An overhead strike to the middle of the forehead, with the blade part of your hand.

Spar: To engage in a continuous flow of meeting others' attacks and initiating one's own.

Sutemi: One interviewee said, "I believe the Japanese meaning of *sutemi* is to give up your life or some kind of sacrifice. It is the forward fall that's done without touching the mat. The difficult part occurs when your entire body is off the ground, your feet are in the air, and someone else is holding onto your wrists."

Throwing: One way of dealing with an attack which involves using the energy of someone's attack to do what looks like throwing them away. In aikido, frequently this results in the person falling hard, or rolling as part of their fall.

Two Step: A way of turning around very rapidly, which is often used as a warm-up.

Uke: One who initiates an "attack," who ends up being thrown, who "receives" the technique.

Ukemi: The "art of falling away from harm." In English, how the attack is referred to. As in, "Are you protecting yourself in your *ukemi?*"

1992 Aikido Today Magazine Dojo Directory

provided courtesy of
Aikido Today Magazine
1420 Claremont Blvd. Suite 111B
Claremont, CA 91711

ALABAMA

Aikido of Birmingham
Greg Faulkner
255 Red Stick Rd.
Pelham, AL 35124
(205) 991–7250

Holy Spirit Yoseikan Aikido
Barry Ackerson
13 31st St. E.
Tuscaloosa, AL 35405
(205) 758–7009

ARKANSAS

Central Arkansas Aikikai
George Jensen
8 Dougherty Hill Rd.
Conway, AR 72032
(501) 327–4925

ARIZONA

Aikido of the Canyonlands
Gail Harold Skinner
3835 N. 2nd Ave.
Tucson, AZ 85705
Home (602) 888–4030

Aikido of Tucson
Barbara Warren
210 W. 5th St. #1
Tucson, AZ 85705
(602) 623–1224

Arizona Aikido of Flagstaff
Bob Frumhoff
823½ W. Aspen #4
Flagstaff, AZ 86001
(602) 779–0563

Arizona Ki Society
Kirk Fowler
7845 E. Evans Rd. Suite F
Scottsdale, AZ 85260
(602) 991–6467

Granite Mountain Aikido
Ben Mancini
HC 30 Box 982
Prescott, AZ 86301
(602) 445–3380

Ki Society Aikido of Southern Arizona
David Shanstrom
7677 E. Speedway Blvd.
Tucson, AZ 85710
(602) 722–0399

Ting Ki Aikido
Peter Ting
609 E. Taylor

Tempe, AZ 85281
(602) 990–8340

CALIFORNIA

ACE Aikido Club
(formerly Ki Aikido Club)
Larry Novick, Ph.D.
Mailing: 2332 S. Bentley Ave.
#202, Los Angeles, CA 90064
(310) 477–0141

Aikido Academy
Francis Takahashi
San Gabriel Japanese
Community Center
5019 N. Encinitas
Temple City, CA 91780
(818) 398–1056

Aikido Arts Center
Jamie Zimron
670 S. Van Ness
San Francisco, CA 94110
(415) 861–6044

Aikido Daiwa
Jack Arnold
12055 ½ Burbank Blvd., N.
Hollywood, CA 91607–1836
(818) 761–9020

**Aikido Federation of California
Yoshinkai**
Shuyokan Dojo
David Dye
PO Box 10962
Costa Mesa, CA 92627
(714) 754–7287

Aikido of Diablo Valley
F. Rowell / S. Dyer / P. Emminger
1231–C Diamond Way
Concord, CA 94520
(510) 676–6763

Aikido of Humboldt Bay
Sandra Schaff
224 G St.
Eureka, CA 95501
(707) 822–7312

Aikido of Livermore Valley
Jim Alvarez
4001 First St. #3
Livermore, CA 94550
(510) 447–4220

Aikido of Los Gatos
Lou Bermingham, Dojo cho
F. Silvey / M. Lipp / J. Adams
Mailing: PO Box 1183
Los Gatos, CA 95031
(408) 354–5314
Training: 123 East Main St.

Aikido Napa
Mark Jones
2516 Laurel
Napa, CA 94558
(707) 257–6639

Aikido of Monterey
Danielle Molles Evans
1251 10th St.
Monterey, CA 93940
(408) 375–8106

Aikido of Point Reyes
David Gamble
PO Box 399
Inverness, CA 94937
(415) 663–8325

Aikido of San Jose
Jack Wada
587 N. Sixth St.
San Jose, CA 95112
(408) 294–3049

Aikido of San Leandro
Patricia Hendricks
1033 MacArthur Blvd.
San Leandro, CA 94577
(510) 430–2518

Aikido Shinbukan
James Bone Friedman
57–B Stillman St.
San Francisco, CA 94107
(415) 777–2833

Aikido Shizenkai
Charles Ii
PO Box 1283
Ridgecrest,CA 93556
(619) 377–4763

Aikido West
Frank Doran
3164 Bay Rd.
Redwood City, CA 94063
(415) 366–9106

Aikido with Ki, Mountain View
Hideki Shiohira, Chief Instructor
c/o International Zen Dojo of
California
2560 Wyandotte St. #A
Mountain View, CA 94043
(415) 969–1731

Aikido with Ki, San Francisco
Hideki Shiohira, Chief Instructor
c/o Social Hall of Konko Church
1755 Laguna St.
San Francisco, CA 94115
(415) 921–5073

Aikido Yoshinkai of California
Sam Combes
1510 S. Euclid Ave.
Anaheim, CA 92802
(714) 774–5730

Aiki Zenshin Dojo
Sunny Skys
42307 Osgood Rd. Unit J
Fremont, CA 94539
(510) 657–5387 or 795–8389

Bay-Marin Aikido
Hans Goto

c/o Terra Linda Rec Center
670 Del Ganado Rd.
San Rafael, CA 94903
(415) 457–5826

Canyon Karate/Aikido
David Alexander
30686 Thousand Oaks Blvd.
Agoura Hills, CA 91301
(818) 889–7898

Chushinkan Dojo
James Nakayama
PO Box 294
Cypress, CA 90630
(714) 772–6363

Claremont Aikido Dojo
Richard A. Sugerman
431 W. Baseline Rd.
Claremont, CA 91711
(714) 985–8292

**Cuesta College Recreation—
Aikido**
Greg Allen Barker
PO Box 8106
San Luis Obispo, CA 93403–8106
(805) 546–3220
Home: (805) 541–4417

**Cultural School—Aikido with
Ki—Goleta Dojo**
Ken and Steve Ota
255 Magnolia Ave.
Goleta, CA 93117
(805) 967–3103

East Bay Aikido
Tom Gambell
1446 Leimert Blvd.
Oakland, CA 94602
(510) 531–0303

Eastshore Aikikai
Elizabeth A. Lynn
Contra Costa College

San Pablo, CA
(510) 237–2711
Mailing: 2101 8th St.
Berkeley, CA 94710

Mendocino Ki Society
Janferie Stone
School and Pine St.
Mendocino, CA 95460
(707) 964–7809

Musubi Dojo
Ronald Rubin / Susan Perry
8181 Monte Vista Ave.
Upland, CA 91786
(714) 920–9929/624–7770

North Bay Aikido
Linda Holiday
708 Washington St.
Santa Cruz, CA 95060
(408) 423–8326

North County Aikikai
Coryl Crane
1051 Arden Dr.
Encinitas, CA 92024
(619) 943–9418

Oceanside Aikikai
Gerald W. Gemmell
2855 Cedar Rd.
Oceanside, CA 92056
(619) 724–2666

Pasadena Aiki Kai
Gene Anderson
Pasadena Japanese Cultural
Center
595 E. Lincoln Ave.
Pasadena, CA 91103
(818) 797–3513

Pinole Aikido
L. Decena
701–C Belmont Way
Pinole, CA 94564
(510) 724–3867

River City Aikido
Herschel Roby
2358 Fruitridge Rd.
Sacramento, CA 95822
(916) 422–7065

Seibukan
Julio Toribio
626 Lighthouse Ave.
Monterey, CA 93940
(408) 375–6797

Sonoma Ki Society
Don Stratton
Sonoma County YMCA
1111 College Ave.
Santa Rosa, CA 95404
(707) 545–9622

**Southern California Ki Society—
Gardena Dojo**
c/o Charles Tomomi Honma
21508 Budlong
Torrance, CA 90502

**Southern California Ki Society—
Goleta Dojo**
The Cultural School
255 S. Magnolia
Goleta, CA 93117
(805) 967–3103

**Southern California Ki Society—
Headquarters**
c/o Masao Shoji
PO Box 3752
Gardena, CA 90247
(310) 514–8834 (info)

**Southern California Ki Society—
Torrance Dojo**
c/o Clarence Chinn
19934 Redbeam
Torrance, CA 90503

Sunset Cliffs Aikido
Bernice Tom
5019 Santa Monica Ave.

San Diego, CA 92107
(619) 222–5085

Tamalpais Aikido
G. Leonard / W. Palmer
/ R. Strozzi Heckler
76 E. Blithedale
Mill Valley, CA 94941
(415) 383–9474

Tenshinkai Aikido Federation
Dang Thong Phong
8536 Westminster Ave.
Westminster, CA 92683
(714) 894–1003

Torrey Pines Aikikai
Walter Muryasz
3986 30th St.
San Diego, CA 92104
(619) 282–5711/ 295–9798

Two Rock Aikido
R. Strozzi Heckler
4101 Middle Two Rock Rd.
Petaluma, CA 94952
(707) 778–6505

Ukiah Aikido
Gayle Fillman
782 Waugh Ln.
Ukiah, CA 95482
(707) 462–5141

**University of California,
Riverside**
Ace D. Atkinson
4444 7th St.
Riverside, CA 92501
(714) 682–2486

**United States Marine Corps
Recruit Depot Aikikai**
Robert Bruce Burns
4365 Montalvo #5
San Diego, CA 92107
(619) 223–1164 or 524–4428

COLORADO

Aikido Nippon Kan
Gaku Homma
988 Cherokee St.
Denver, CO 80204
(303) 595–8256

Ai to Heiwa (Love & Peace)
Stephan Varjan
4214 E. Colfax Ave.
Denver, CO 80220
(303) 329–6408

Aikido of Creston
Dan Retuta
PO Box 156
Creston, CO 81131
(719) 256–4036

Boulder Aikikai
Hiroshi Ikeda
4770 Pearl St. Units B & C
Boulder, CO 80301
(303) 444–7721

Pike's Peak Aikikai
Wayne Perkins
3425–H Van Teylingen Dr.,
Colorado Springs, CO 80917
(719) 574–7420

Rocky Mountain Aikikai
S. M. (Jack) Ross
23 Lindenwood Dr.
Littleton, CO 80120
(303) 795–7158

**Rocky Mountain Ki Society,
Boulder**
Goodson Recreation Center
Russell Jones
2400 30th St., Box 18
Boulder, CO 80306
(303) 442–0505

Rocky Mountain Ki Society
CATS Gym

Russell Jones
5455 W. 38th Ave.
Denver, CO 80212
(303)425–0988

CONNECTICUT

Aikido Institute of New England
Skip Rackmill
181 W. Mountain Rd.
W. Simsbury, CT 06092
(203) 651–8352

Aikido of Fairfield County
Ray Farinato
14 Creeping Hemlock Dr.
Norwalk, CT 06851
(203) 846–6944

Aikido of Litchfield County
John Hrabushi
51 Weekeepeemee Rd.
Woodbury, CT 06798
(203) 777–2940

DELAWARE

New Castle County Aikikai
Zenko Okimura, Shidoin
118 Astro Shopping Center
Newark, DE 19711
(302) 738–6466 or 737–6278

FLORIDA

Aikido Academy of Self-Defense
Steven A. Weber
4553 Grand Blvd.
New Port Richey, FL 34652
(813) 849–8800

Cocoa Beach Aikikai
John B. Thompson
220 S. 14th St.
Cocoa Beach, FL 32931
(407) 783–8373

Gainesville Kodokai Aikido
1215 N.W. 5th Ave.
Gainesville, FL 32601
(904) 378–7131

International Budo Ryokukai
Dennis Fritchie
686 S.E. Monterey Rd.
Stuart, FL 34995
(407) 288–2010

Issho Ni Ryu Dojo
Terrenyce J. Cooper
Westside Karate & Aikido Dojo
5533 West Kinett Blvd.
Jacksonville, FL 32210
(904) 779–7767

International Karate Center
Neal Hummerstone
2700 Enterprise Rd.
Orange City, FL 32763
(904) 774–7555

Melbourne Aikikai Kenjutsukai
Anthony Graziano
950 Pinetree Dr.
Indian Harbor Beach, FL 32937
(407) 777–1011

Ohrikai Dojo
Timothy M. Dudley
4523 30th St. W. Unit 104
Bradenton, FL 34207
(813) 753–7212

Orlando Kodokai Aikido
Bill Dennis / Eddie Castro
Columbus Center
4625 Middlebrook Rd.
Orlando, FL 32811
(407) 898–9305

Palm Beach Aikikai
Richard Wagener
Jewish Community Center
3151 North Military Trail

W. Palm Beach, FL 33407
(407) 881–5717

St. Petersburg Aikikai
John Messores
2728 18th Ave. N.
St. Petersburg, FL 33713
(813) 321–7411

Sarasota Aikikai
Steve McPeck
2100 20th St.
Sarasota, FL 34234
(813) 365–6366 or 365–5307

Tampa Aikikai
Dan Fernandez
16603 Plum Rose Ct.
Tampa, FL 33618
(813) 254–4505 (day) or
960–1651 (evening)

**University of Central Florida
Aikido Club**
Edward Baker / Peter Easton
Education Bldg.
Multipurpose Rm., UCF
Orlando, FL 32816
(407) 294–9437
Mailing address:
3728 Okeechobee Circle
Casselberry, FL 32707

Also

Martial Arts Academy
1630 South Orlando Ave.
Maitland, FL 32751
(407) 740–0092

GEORGIA

Savannah Aikido-Kai
604 Leaning Oaks Dr.
Savannah, GA 31410
(912) 897–0922

HAWAII

Hawaii Aikido Federation
PO Box 26497
Honolulu, HI 96825–0800

Kailua Aikido Club
Robert Kubo
c/o Windward YMCA
1200 Kailua Rd.
Kailua, HI 96734
(808) 235–1486

Pearl City Aikido Club
Donald Moriyama
PO Box 1567
Pearl City, HI 96782
(808) 455–7000 or 488–6747

Shizendo Aiki-waza
(division of Shizendo Kanno
Kanwa Kai)
Hideo M. Kimura
Young Buddhists Assn.
1710 Pali Hwy.
Honolulu, HI 96813
(808) 537–6954 or 671–1422

IDAHO

Aikido of Idaho
Bill Mission / Curtis L. V. Adams,
M.D.
1512 N. 10th St.
Boise, ID 83702
(208) 387–0410

ILLINOIS

American Aikido Society
Keith Benedix
7751 W. Bryn Mawr
Chicago, IL 60631
(312) 763–1556

Aikido Association of America
Fumio Toyoda, Shihan
1016 W. Belmont Ave.

Chicago, IL 60657
(312) 525–3141
Fax: (312) 525–5916

Beecher Aikikai
Wendy Whited
700 Penfield
Beecher, IL 60401
(708) 946–6614

Chicago Aikikai
Kevin Choate
1627 W. Howard St.
Chicago, IL 60626
(312) 743–0618

Illinois State University Aikido Program
Dr. Jeffrey B. Hecht
ISU Campus, Recreation Services
500 North Beach
Normal, IL 61761
(309) 438–PLAY

Midwest Aikido Center
Akira Tohei
3249 N. Ashland Ave.
Chicago, IL 60657
(312) 477–0123

Shugakukan Dojo
Gilbert James
4702 S. Western
Chicago, IL 60609
(312) 324–3465 (evening)

INDIANA

Aikido Yoshinkan of Indianapolis
C. Howey / E. Dysarz / J. Todd
2131 E. 54th St. #4
Indianapolis, IN 46220
(317) 251–2070

Aikido Yoshinkai of Kokomo
Gregory J. Saul
Kokomo Sports Center
111 Southway Blvd.

Kokomo, IN 46901
(317) 455–0167

Fort Wayne Aikido Dojo
Jane Berghoff
2000 N. Wells St. (YWCA)
Fort Wayne, IN 46808
(219) 749–6402

Indiana University Tomiki Aikido
Paul Smith
7487 N. John Young Rd.
Unionville, IN 47468
(812) 336–8036

Ki-Baru Dojo
George Bevins
6160 E. 116th St.
Fishers, IN 46038
(317) 578–9283

Indiana Univ. Ueshiba Aikido Club
Kim Sommer
3905 W. 3rd #16
Bloomington, IN 47403
(812) 339–4746

KANSAS

Salina Aikido Club
Peter Kimble
2613 Argonne Dr.
Salina, KS 67401
(913) 825–6643
Class at Memorial Hall Gym, 9th and Ash.

KENTUCKY

Aikido of Louisville, Inc.
Jim Ragan / Tony Graziano
c/o Tony Graziano
3101 Bardstown Rd.
Louisville, KY 40205
(502) 458–0858 or 451–1962

Aikido of Owensboro
Daniel Caslin
801 Old Hartford Rd.
Owensboro, KY 42302
(502) 683–8814
Dojo currently located at the
Triplett School.

UK Aikido Club
Tony Graziano
c/o Harry Sloan
794 Glendover Ct.
Lexington, KY 40502
(606) 269–4305

LOUISIANA

Gentle Wind Dojo
Becky Sexton
11686 Florida Blvd.
Baton Rouge, LA 70815
(504) 272–8500

Greater New Orleans Aikikai
Hayward Gaude
931 Canal St. #328
New Orleans, LA 70112
(504) 568–9566
Classes held at Loyola University.

New Orleans Aikido Club
Larry Pohlman
c/o Institute of Martial Arts
732 Atherton
Metairie, LA 70001
(504) 466–3523

MARYLAND

Aikido of Maryland, Inc
John C. Goss Jr.
8620 Belair Rd.
Perry Hall, MD 21236
(410) 529–5222

MASSACHUSETTS

Aikido of Springfield
Lorraine DiAnne
145 Chestnut St.
Springfield, MA 01105
(413) 731–6661

Bushido-Kai
Tony Annesi
21 Blandin Ave.
Framingham, MA 01701
(508) 879–7622

Martha's Vineyard Aikido Club
Sean Conley
10 Elias Ln.
West Tisbury, MA 02575
(508) 693–3953 (eve)

Shobu Aikido of Boston
William Gleason
17 Station St.
Brookline Village, MA 02146
(617) 734–3208 or 964–9571

Shodokan Dojo
B. J. Mulligan
89 Canal St.
Salem, MA 01970
(508) 744–1232

Zen Dojo of Central MA
Dr. E. Haupt
Setsudo Farm
Rutland, MA 01543
(508) 886–4424

MICHIGAN

**Aikido Training Center of
Detroit**
(Shi Sei Kan Dojo)
Herman Hurst
18279 Livernois Ave.
Detroit, MI 48221
(313) 863–9522

International Budo Ryokukai
Katsumi Niikura
2133 15 Mile Rd.
Sterling Heights, MI 48077
(313) 978–8332

International Budo Ryokukai
Robert Aldis
Richmond High School
Richmond, MI 48062
(313) 320–6397

Lapeer Aikido Club
Greg Garbulinski
2929 Haines Rd.
Lapeer, MI 48446
(313) 667–3602

Michigan Athletic Club Aikido
Kate Dernocoeur
c/o 2555 Oakwood S.E.
Grand Rapids, MI 49506
(616) 957–7998

Michigan Tech Aikido Club
Mark Campbell-Olszewski
214 Hubbell St.
Houghton, MI 49931
(906) 482–3551

MINNESOTA

Aikido Yoshinkai Minneapolis-
St. Paul
Alvin McClure
194 E. 6th St.
St. Paul, MN 55101
(612) 889–2098

MISSISSIPPI

Eight Winds Aikido Society
Steve Wade / Carmen Pelusi
1800 Still Water Dr.
Gautier, MS 39553
(601) 497–9750, 497–5055,
497–3451

MISSOURI

Central Missouri State
University Aikikai
Doris Evans
602 Springridge Rd. #B–15
Warrensburg, MO 64093
(816) 429–2218

Missouri Aikikai
Eric M. Henkels
6006 Pershing
St. Louis, MO 63112
(314) 361–2346
Mailing address: Eric M. Henkels
c/o Vision Point Management
4937 Laclede
St. Louis, MO 63108

St. Louis Ki Society
Mark Rubbert
6006 Pershing Ave.
St. Louis, MO 63112
(314) 726–5070

Springfield Aikido School
Jeff League
Box 460, RR 2
Fair Grove, MO 65648
(417) 759–2942

MONTANA

Glacier Aiki Kai
Walther G. Von Krenner
PO Box 1338
Kalispell, MT 59903–1338
(406) 755–2745

Havre Aikido Club
Mark Earnhardt
195 78th Ave. W.
Havre, MT 59501
(406) 265–5002

Last Chance Aikido
Whitney Hibbard
9 Placer Ave.

Helena, MT 59601
(406) 443–3911

Missoula Aikikai
Raso Hultgren
2304 Rattlesnake Dr.
Missoula, MT 59802
(406) 542–3810 or 728–8787
Dojo: 208 E. Main (upstairs)

NEVADA

Las Vegas Aikikai
Gregory Hofler
3036 S. Valley View
Las Vegas, NV 89102
(702) 870–0704 or 433–1575

Reno Aikido Co-op
Wolfgang Baumgartner
195 N. Edison Way #10
Reno, NV 89502
(702) 856–5977

NEW HAMPSHIRE

Aiki Budokai New Hampshire
Thom Pristow
Dartmouth College
Hanover, NH 03755
(603) 989–5670

Kazoku Dojo
Michael Donnelly
People's Fitness
20 Pleasant St.
Concord, NH 03301
(603) 735–5998

Morningstar Aikikai
Joseph Caulfield Esq.
PO Box 147
Lyndeborough, NH 03082
(603) 654–5730

NEW JERSEY

Agatsu Dojos
R. Crane / K. Crane
31 South Whitehorse Pike
Stratford, NJ 08084
(609) 435–2667

Aikido Institute of Asian Studies
Howard R. Biffson
1043 Shore Rd.
Linwood, NJ 08221
(609) 927–4124

Aikido Kokikai Lambertville
Ken Blackwell
and Princeton Aikido Kokikai
Sheila Blackwell
1312 Scenic Dr.
W. Trenton, NJ 08628
(609) 883–0595

Aikido Kokikai Princeton
Dan McDougall
12 Crusher Rd.
Hopewell, NJ 08525
(609) 466–3779

Aikido Kokikai Princeton University
Gary Snyder
12 Pond Ct.
Belle Mead, NJ 08502
(908) 359–4661

Applied Martial Art Concepts, Inc.
Jose A. Rua, M.A., Sr. Branch Instructor
187 Washington Ave.
Fort Lee, NJ 07024
(201) 944–0612

Long Beach Island Aikikai
Chester S. Griffin
St. Francis Community Center
4700 Long Beach Blvd.

Long Beach Township, NJ 08008
(609) 492–4064

Vineland Aikikai
Peter Tamagni
c/o 2161 Pennsylvania Ave.
Millville, NJ 08332
(609) 327–2475

NEW MEXICO

Aikido Institute of New Mexico
1542 Cerrillos Rd.
Santa Fe, NM 87501
(505) 988–7173

Aikido of Santa Fe
Takashi Tokunaga
1807 2nd St. #16
Santa Fe, NM 87501
(505) 983–9115

Jiyushinkai Shoshin Dojo
Shihan C. E. Clark / B. Roybal /
P. Tawada
3018 Cielo Ct.
Santa Fe, NM 87505
(505) 438–9714

Roninkai Aikido
Damon Apodaca
2019 Pinon St.
Santa Fe, NM 87501
(505) 690–0606

Southwester Aikikai
Kris Varjan
317 Ojo de la Vaca
Santa Fe, NM 87505

**University of New Mexico
Aikido Club**
Lorina and Penryn
PO Box 9360
Albuquerque, NM 87119
(505) 281–5220

NEW YORK

Aikido of Central New York
Mr. Yousuf Mehter
2740 Erie Blvd. E.
Syracuse, NY 13224
(315) 449–2332

Aikido of Nassau County
Collings / Gabriel / Marcus /
Nemeth
26 Clinton Ave.
Valley Stream, NY 11580
(516) 561–8040

Aikido of Staten Island
Ralph Wemberly
420 Targee St.
Staten Island, NY 10304
(718) 442–5125

Aiki New York
John A. Zenkewich
213 Westchester Ave.
Yonkers, NY 10707
(914) 793–1652

Jikishinkan Dojo
Shaku J. Jarman
211 Smith St.
Brooklyn, NY 11201
(718) 488–9511

Long Island Aikido Association
E. Hagihara
c/o Yanagi Martial Arts
425 Conklin Ave.
Farmingdale, NY 11735
(516) 431–7713

New York Aikido Club
(aka Bond Street Dojo)
Kang / Jordan / Nisson
49 Bond St., New York, NY 10012
(212) 477–0899 after 6 PM

East Village (near NYU)
New York Ki Society
Shizuo Imaizumi
416 W. 14th St., 4th floor
New York, NY 10014
(212) 691–1378

Seidokan of New York
James Wallace
322 N. Aurora St.
Ithaca, NY 14850
(607) 277–6410

Woodstock Aikido
Harvey Konigsberg
PO Box 549
Woodstock, NY 12498
(914) 679–9166

NORTH CAROLINA

Aikido of Charlotte
Dennis Main
9415 Peckham Rye Rd.
Charlotte, NC 28227
(704) 545–8584
Dojo address: Martial Arts
Training Institute
1607–G Montford Drive
Charlotte, NC 28227

The Martial Arts Center
John LaMont
328 W. Morgan St.
Raleigh, NC 27601
(919) 834–1133

OHIO

Aikido of Cleveland
Linda Lee Vecchio
6727 Olde Field Court
Mentor, OH 44060–3994
Home: (216) 951–3023
Work: (216) 953–7111

Aikido of Cincinnati
Charlie McGinnis
1403 Central Parkway, 4th floor
Cincinnati, OH 45214
(513) 651–AIKI

Circle of Harmony
Michael and Mary Pabst
160 W. Case Street (rear)
Powell, OH 43065
(614) 792–6424

Columbus Aikikai
Frank Hreha / Claude Geeroms
3840 Lacon Rd. #4
Hilliard, OH 43026
Home: (614) 851–0154
Dojo: (614) 771–5599

Oberlin Aikikai
Guy H. Haskell
262 N. Main St.
Oberlin, OH 44074
(216) 775–8639

OKLAHOMA

Shobu Aiki Dojo
Steve Duncan
2600 N. Independence
PO Box 76262
Oklahoma City, OK 73147
(405) 949–5646

Tulsa Aikido Club
Michael Pollack
1926 E. 36th St.
Tulsa, OK 74105
(918) 748–8990

OREGON

Aikido of Ashland
Michael Friedl
201 Alicia St.
Ashland, OR 97520
(503) 482–3191

Aikido Northwest
Craig Fife / Elizabeth Hendricks
19057 S.W. Olson Ave.
Lake Oswego, OR 97034
(503) 638–4879

Pacific Rim Martial Arts Academy
James Garrison
4265–A S.W. Cedar Hills Blvd.
Beaverton, OR 97005
(503) 626–3869

PENNSYLVANIA

Aikido Association of North America (AANA)
Yukio Utada
5836 Henry Ave.
Philadelphia, PA 19128
(215) 483–3000

Aikido Kinokawa
Byron M. Mellinger
600 Penn Ave.
West Reading, PA 19611
(215) 372–1235

Aikido Kokikai Headquarters
Shuji Maruyama
6907 Rising Sun Ave.
Philadelphia, PA 19111
(215) 728–9380

Lehigh Valley Aikido Club
Minh Nguyen
1008 W. North St.
Bethlehem, PA 18018
(215) 868–6176

Philadelphia Ki Society
Hal Abramson
University of PA Ki-Aikido Club
314 S. Fawn St.
Philadelphia, PA 19107
(215) 732–8425

Three Rivers Aikikai
c/o David Raffo
7124 Card Ln.
Pittsburgh, PA 15208
(412) 243–2170

SOUTH CAROLINA

Mike Sanders Aikido & Jujitsu Dojo
Mike Sanders
1831 Wade Hampton Blvd.
Greenville, SC 29609
(803) 292–3453

Mt. Pleasant Aikido
Alan Jackson
1446 Barbara St.
Mt. Pleasant, SC 29464
Home: (803) 884–7099
Work: (803) 723–7837

TEXAS

Aikido of Austin
Jo Birdsong
218 W. 4th St.
Austin, TX 78701
(512) 472–AIKI (2454)

Austin Ki Aikido Center
K. Ferland / J. Kearns / L. Crane
211 W. North Loop
Austin, TX 78757
(512) 459–9249

Dallas Aikido Club
Jack Bieler
4135 Polaris #3086
Irving, TX 75038
(214) 570–1388

Jinshinkan Dojo
Dr. Fred Phillips
2700 W. Anderston Lane #301
Austin, TX 78759
(512) 250–9309

San Antonio Aikikai
Kevin Templer
7520 Portranco Rd. #604
San Antonio, TX 78251
(512) 520–AIKI

Southwestern Aikido Institute, Inc.
Bill Sosa
726 W. Jefferson Blvd.
Dallas, TX 75208
(214) 823–4491

VERMONT

Aikido of Montpelier
Sara Norton
174 River St.
Montpelier, VT 05602
(802) 454–8550

Vermont Aikido
Hugh Young
274 North Winooski Ave.
Burlington, VT 05401
(802) 862–9785

VIRGINIA

Aikido of Arlington
Don Lyon
1301 S. Scott St.
Arlington, VA 22204
(703) 979–5131

Aikido of Northern VA
Robert Galeone
1180-A Pendleton
Alexandria, VA 22314
(703) 739–2620
Mailing: 626 Ritchie Ave.
Silver Spring, MD 20910

Virginia Ki Society
George Simcox
2723A Merrilee Dr.
Merrifield, VA 22116

Mailing: PO Box 2351
Merrifield, VA 22116

WASHINGTON

Aikido Eastside
George S. Ledyard
13410 S.E. 32nd St.
Bellevue, WA 98005
(206) 868–1902

Aikido Kokikai Seattle
Jonathan Bannister
PO Box 70292
Seattle, WA 98107
(206) 789–9511

Aikido, Port Townsend
Paul Becker
Mailing: 1408 Adams St.
Port Townsend, WA 98368
(206) 385–2977

Defense Arts Academy
Curt Thompson
12907 E. Sprague
Spokane, WA 99216
(509) 926–0819

Emerald City Aikido
Joanne Veneziano
604 19th Ave. E.
Seattle, WA 98112
(206) 323–2322

Kannagara Dojo
K. Barrish
17720 State Rd. 92
Granite Falls, WA 98252
(206) 691–6389

Seattle Aikikai
Bruce Bookman
7700 Aurora Ave. N.
Seattle, WA 98103
(206) 525–4032

WASHINGTON, D.C.

Aikido Shobukan Dojo
M. Saotome
421 Butternut St. N.W.
Washington, DC 20012
(202) 829–4202

WISCONSIN

Green Bay Aikikai
Micah O'Malley
YWCA, 230 S. Madison St.
Green Bay, WI 54301
(414) 336–7561
also YMCA (235 North Jefferson St.)

Milwaukee Aikido Club
Norio Mamura
2235 S. Kinnickinnic Ave.
Milwaukee, WI 53207
(414) 744–9220

OUTSIDE THE U.S.

BRAZIL

Instituto Takemussu
Wagner Bull
Rua Jussara, 145 CEP 04137
Sao Paulo
(011) 581 62 41/275 47 34

CANADA

Aikido de la Montagne
Claude Berthiaume
3734 Ave du Parc
Montreal, Quebec H2X 2J1
(514) 845–2729

Aikikai de Montreal
Massimo di Villadorata
4510 St. Denis
Montreal, Quebec H2J 2G5
(514) 845–5971

AYC-Scarborough Dojo
Debra McAllister / Eric Sheffield
3600 Kingston Rd.
Scarborough, Ontario M1P 4N7
(416) 234–5289

AYC-Scarborough Dojo at Scarborough Village Recreation Centre
Metropolitan Toronto:
Cambridge Ki-Aikido Society
Mike Hogan
PO Box 454
Cambridge, Ontario N8W 1B3
(519) 740–6894

Chudokan Aikido Dojo
Kevin Blok
1089 Tecumseh Rd. E.
Windsor, Ontario N9J 1C1
(519) 253–6667 (d)
978–1263 (inst)

Kingston Ki Society
Rev. Bill Bickford
114 Nicholson Crescent,
Amherstview, Ontario K7N IXI
(613) 384–0423

Maple Ridge Yoshinkan Aikido
Keith Taylor
1410 Toronto Pl.
Port Coquitlam, BC U3B 2T7
(604) 944–9329

Pacific Aikido Kensankai
Michael Linehan
3350 Victoria, Rm. 4
Vancouver, BC V5N 5L4
(604) 874–8641
Mail: Box 65955, STN F

Renbukan Aikido Club
James and Susan Jeannette
c/o 3307 Academy Dr.
Windsor, Ontario N9E 2H7
Phone/Fax: (519) 966–2297

FRANCE

ACN Aikido
Michel Becart
1 rue Duvergier
Paris 75019
(331) 40 35 21 49 or 40 35 45 45

GCERCCE–EIAMS
M. Michel Soulenq
16 rue du Square Carpeaux
75018 Paris
(33) 1 44 85 97 25

GERMANY

Aikido Institut Munchen
Adriano Trevisan
Preysingstr 28
8000 Munchen 80
089 4485846 or 484587

HOLLAND

Aikido School Ma-ai
Ad Van Dun
Fr Romanusweg 60
6221–AH Maastricht
(043) 217–213/438–426

Shin Ryu Kai Aikido Nederland
Isaac Reawaru, Wilbert K. Sluiter
c/o Lopikstreet 1, 2456 EN
The Hague
070–3670653

HONG KONG

**The Hong Kong Aikido
Association**
Mr. Kenneth Cottier, President
Mr. Michael Leung, Chairman
Kowloon Park Indoor Gymnasium
Kowloon
(852) 803–2860

JAPAN

Ibaraki Aikido Shuren Dojo
(aka Iwama Dojo)
Morihiro Saito
26 Yoshioka, Iwama-machi
Nishi-Ibaraki-gun
Ibaraki-ken 319–02
0299–453788

Keijutsukai Aikido
Thomas Makiyama
Shimbashi Shinwa Bldg. 4F, 5–15
4–Chome, Shimbashi Minato,
Tokyo 105
(03) 5472–5181/2
Fax: (03) 5472–5180

**Tohoku Fukushi University
Aikido Club**
John Stevens
Kunimi 1–8–1, Aoba-ku
Sendai 981
Fax: 022–273–5322

SWEDEN

Wasa Aikido Dojo
Henrik Blomdahl
Hagagatan 31, 5, S–11347,
Stockholm
08–325249

Women's Dojo Directory

provided courtesy of
Fighting Women News
6741 Tung Ave. West
Theodore, Alabama 36582

Directory

  a: all woman instructors

  b: at least one woman instructor

  c: no woman instructor

  d: all classes women only

  e: some classes women only

  f: no classes women only

  g: self-defense stressed

  h: self-defense included

  i: self-defense not stressed

  j: household discounts

  k: sliding scale

  l: no discounts

m: childcare available

  n: limited childcare

  o: no childcare

  p: children's classes

  q: children take regular classes

  r: no children's classes

  s: differently-abled
    accommodated

  t: wheelchair accessible

  *: leave message

ALABAMA

Theodore Tae Kwon Do, Inc.
Debra Pettis
6741 Tung Ave. W.
Theodore, AL 36582
(205) 653–0549
Tae Kwon Do
bfgj

CALIFORNIA

Patricia Giggansla
Commission on Assaults Against
Women
543 N. Fairfax Ave.
Los Angeles, CA 90036
(213) 462–1281
adgks

**Women's Self-Defense of
Canoga Park**
Rocl Arsenian
22926 Slagg St.
West Hills, CA 91304
(818) 887–5427
Kyokushinkai
cdg

Topanga Valley Karate School
21512 Sherman Wy.
Topanga, CA 90290
(818) 883–4282
Shofokan & Kobu-jitsu
Self-defense
bfgjpt*

KarateWomen School of
Movement and Martial Arts
12804 Venice Blvd.
Los Angeles, CA 90066
(310) 398–5539
Shonn-ryu karate
afhpa

Kwmposilama Self-Defense
School
c/o Clara E. Minor
1515 Mission St.
Santa Cruz, CA 95060
(408) 458–0900
begjkmpst

Ronindojo
1162 Folsom
San Francisco, CA 94103
(415) 695–0735
American kenpo karate
abdkor

FLORIDA

Sansei South Goju Karate
Master Rusell P. Rogg
18495 South Dixie Hwy.
Miami, FL 33157
(305) 238–7850
Shendo Goju Ryu
beghjknpst

ILLINOIS

Chimera Self-Defense, Inc.
Penny Wilson
59 E. Van Buren #714
Chicago, IL 60605
(312)939–5341
Self-defense for women and girls
(12 yrs +)
adgkors*

INDIANA

Tai Chi Chu'an Assn. of IN, Inc.
Laura Stone, President
P.O. Box 1834
Bloomington, IN 47402
(812) 332–9911
Tai chi chu'an, yoga
bfh

MARYLAND

D.C. Self-Defense Karate Assn.
Carol Middleton
701 Richmond Ave.
Silver Spring, MD 20901
(301) 589–1349
Tae kwon do
behjkopsi

MASSACHUSETTS

Amherst Martial Arts
c/o Annie Schwarz
111 Sunderland Rd.
Amherst, MA 01002
(413) 549–7515
Tae kwon do
aehjp

Vallet Women's Martial Arts, Inc.
Janet Aalfs
P.O. Box 1064
One Cottage St.
Easthampton, MA 01027
(413) 527–0101
Shun–ryu Karate, Modem Amis
adgknpst*

MICHIGAN

Korean Martial Arts Institute
P.O. Box 631
Lapser, MI 48446
(313) 667–2101
Tae Kwon Do
bfhjkops

Okinawan Karate Club
Barbara Christensen
1607 Anderson
Ann Arbor, MI 48103
(313)554–2640
Shorin-ryu karate
adikorsi

Movement Arts
Joan Nelson, director
230 Bingham
Lansing, MI 48912
(517)485–3668
afh

MINNESOTA

West Bank Tai Chi Chung
Phyllis Calph
504 Cedar Ave. South, 2nd floor
Minneapolis, MN 55454
(612) 333–8635
·(yang) Tai Chi Chuan
bh

NEW YORK

New World Center of Martial Arts
Mary Bogold
30 Comet St.
Buffalo, NY 14216
(716) 875–1800
behiopl°

Japanese Swordsmanship Society
P.O. Box 1116
Rockefeller Center Station
New York, NY 10185
(212) 891–2891
Laido, jodo, kendo, naginata
bfi

Kidojo
598 Hertel Ave.
Buffalo, NY 14207
(716) 875–2061

Isshinryu Karate—Carol Froelich
Akido—Maritza Ballen
aeghops

Stephen J. Gamma's School of Self-Defense
(D.B.A. Stephen J. Gamma Productions)
P.O. Box 486
Walden, NY 12586
(914) 778–1562
cfgst

NORTH CAROLINA

Safe Skills Center
P.O. Box 61643
Durham, NC 27715
(919) 682–7262

OHIO

Ohio Women Martial Artists
Columbus, OH 43202
(614) 268–6873
Tae Kwon Do, Amis, Street Self-defense
aegnps

OREGON

One With Heart Poekoelan
42313 SE Hawthorne Blvd.
Portland, OR 97215
(503)231–1999
Indonesian Kung Fu, Women's self-defense
gjp

World Oriental Martial Arts Federation
Master James R. Garrison
12246 NW Kearny St.
Portland, OR 97229

PENNSYLVANIA

Galetti's Tae Kwon Do, Inc.
Teresa Galetti, 3rd Dan
P.O. Box 222
Plymouth Meeting, PA 19462
(215) 825–3559
Tae Kwon Do
bfhjoqs*

WISCONSIN

American Martial Arts Academy
Joanne Nelson/owner-instructor
104 Trunkline Rd.
P.O. Box 1034
Wautoma, WI 54982
Tae Kwon Do
bjhoqs

Peace Seeker Martial Arts for Women
Lisa Amacher
132 N. George St.
Whitewater, WI 53190
(414) 473–7429
adgjkoqst*

OUTSIDE THE UNITED STATES

CANADA

Karate for Women
c/o Joni Miller
3091 W. 15th
Vancouver, BC
Canada V6K 3A5
(604) 734–9816*
ahpq

W.E.S.T.

Women Educating in Self-Defense Training
Alice MacPherson
2349 St. Catherines St.
Vancouver, B.C. V5T 3X8
(604) 876–6390

GERMANY

Fraueninbewegung Tae Kwondo and Self-Defense School
Sunny Graff
Gauss–Str. 12 6000
Frankfurt 1
069–4950710
06527–2103*

SWITZERLAND

Moo Sul Kwan—Martial Arts School
Dr. Barbara Schaer
Postfach 107
CH-6826 Riva San Vitale
(091) 48–3651
Tae Kwon Do

Acknowledgments

Thanks to the women who told me their stories. They were, without exception, unfailingly generous, courteous, patient, and articulate.

Thanks to Roberta Cairney for patient and good-humored legal advice. Thanks to Wendy Ellen Ledger for transcription and writing assistance, Cheryl Reinhardt for aikido instruction, Jan Watson for the interior photographs, Schuyler Pescada for the cover photo, and the many other photographers who helped along the way. Thanks to Matthew Siegel for general coaching.

Thanks to Alexa Eurich, Annie Fox, David Fox, Shea Godwin, Tom Hassett, Sarah Jurick, Danika Lew, Judith Lucero, Hilary Macht, Janine Pitot, Larri Rosser, Marion Sorenson, Joan Wolff, and Renée Alfandary for proofreading and support.

Thanks to Karen Davis, Jim Godfrey, Madelyn Hackett, Jeannie Benjamin, Stephen Booth, Linda Guadagnoli, Claire Rothenberg, Steve Purcell, Dave Grossman, Melanie Mociun, Hal Barwood, Marion Rosen, Carol Adler, David Taylor, Maureen Murphy, Allan Stone, and Bill Sarnoff for important general support.

Thanks to the many people in the martial arts community who gave of their time and expertise, especially Peter Brown, Ray Chan, Priscilla Curry, Larry Ohrman, Linda Holliday, Betsy Hill, David Gamble, Megan Reisel, and Denise Berry.

Grateful acknowledgment is made to Debra L. Pettis of *Fighting Woman News* and Susan Perry of *Aikido Today Magazine* for their comprehensive international lists of Aikido and women's dojos.

Andrew Gelman provided outstanding technical support and assistance including creating a way to tape-record the phone interviews and hand-dyeing his old karate belt four colors of blue for me when I passed the blue belt exam.

Thanks to my fabulous Grandma, Ruth Stone, to my Mom (without her help, none of this would have been possible), and to my beloved sister, Alicia.

Thanks to those whom I forgot to mention.